At Home, At War

At Home, At War

Domesticity and World War I
in American Literature

Jennifer Haytock

The Ohio State University Press
Columbus

Library of Congress Cataloging-in-Publication Data

Haytock, Jennifer Anne.
    At home, at war : domesticity and World War I in American literature /
Jennifer Haytock.
        p. cm.
Includes bibliographical references and index.
    ISBN 0-8142-0932-7 (alk. paper)
    1. American fiction—20th century—History and criticism. 2. World
War, 1914–1918—United States—Literature and the war. 3. Domestic
fiction, American—History and criticism. 4. War stories,
American—History and criticism. 5. Home in literature. 6. War in
literature. I. Title.
    PS374.W65H39 2003
    813.'509358—dc21

                                                                2002156391

Cover design by Dan O'Dair.
Printed by Thomson-Shore, Inc.

The paper used in this publication meets the minimum requirements of
the American National Standard for Information Sciences—Permanence
of Paper for Printed Library Materials. ANSI Z39.48-1992.

9 8 7 6 5 4 3 2 1

To my parents, Ben and Nancy

Contents

Preface
Of Genre and Gender:
The "Domestic Novel" and the
"War Novel"

In her 1999 Alexander lecture series *Women's Lives: The View from the Threshold*, Carolyn Heilbrun writes, "Feminists . . . look precisely for what can be changed, ought to be changed, must be changed, for what has wrongly and for too long . . . been considered immutable." Feminists and women writers work from a liminal position, she argues, "an in-between-ness" from which they can find and use power (98). Seeing connections between that which has been categorically isolated and hierarchically valued—value distributed along gender lines—is an important feminist project, one that we must not assume, even after approximately thirty years of feminist literary study, has been completed. Although the canon wars have raised provocative questions and altered what we teach and what we study, we can still find a great many pockets and gaps where entrenched ways of looking at literature remain; these pockets can illuminate both women's and men's writing as well as the activity of literary criticism. As we move into the twenty-first century, we have a chance to establish a critical ground in which gender can become a fruitful, energetic tool of criticism and less an evaluative gauge. An ongoing investigation of past and present critical practices is necessary to allow us to see what we have, in Heilbrun's words, "wrongly" viewed as "immutable."

In *At Home, At War*, I examine two categories of American literature that seem immutably separate and clearly gendered: the domestic novel and the war novel. Heilbrun's view of the feminist project as liminal provides a space from which to look at these novels together. Questioning these established categories demonstrates that feminist study can reveal much not only about women's lives and women's writing but also about men's lives and their relationship to the domestic world and to writing about the home.

Over the past thirty years, domestic writing—once virtually ignored by the literary community—has taken its place as a recognized and valued form of American literature. The process through which this movement has occurred demonstrates changes in literary criticism and positions us to approach literature in still further directions. In the early 1980s, Nina Baym and Annette Kolodny, as well as other feminist critics, explored the reasons that much literature by women has been consistently excluded from the literary canon. In looking at American literary history, Baym shows that "women have not written the kind of work that we call 'excellent'" (1985, 64) because the way we define "excellent" is culturally determined. Furthermore, she argues, in the nineteenth century and earlier, "excellent" writing meant "American" literature, and to express Americanness writers depicted a (usually male) individual battling the forces of nature and of society, both figured—contrastingly—as feminine. "American" literature also had to invoke criticism against the consensus, and male critics tended "to assume that [women's] gender made them part of the consensus in a way that prevented them from partaking in the criticism" (69). This assumption about women's placid acceptance of the society in which they lived, however, can be seen to be false, if one reads women's texts seriously.

Thus the issue of how we read has a singular importance. In "A Map for Rereading: Gender and the Interpretation of Literary Texts," Kolodny deconstructs Harold Bloom's argument about the creation of the literary canon and explores its implications for women's writing (1985b). Whereas Bloom claims that the canon was formed by a body of writers reading the same material and drawing on it to form a collective understanding of literature and meaning, Kolodny points out that, for quite some time, women writers were not educated as their fellow male writers were. Even after women began receiving a standard education, their experiences still differed widely from men's; thus, "from the 1850s on, in America at least, the meanings 'wandering around between texts' were wandering around somewhat different groups of texts where male and female readers were concerned" (49). Because reading, as Kolodny argues, is a culturally learned and defined activity, male readers were unprepared to decipher the symbolic meaning found in women's texts: "Symbolic representations, in other words, depend on a fund of shared recognition and potential inference" (58). In "Dancing through the Minefield," Kolodny points out that if language is gender informed, as many critics now understand it to be, "male readers who find themselves outside of and unfamiliar with the symbolic systems that constitute female experience in women's writing will necessarily dismiss those systems as undecipherable, meaningless, or trivial" (1985a, 148). Women's writing, claims Kolodny, failed to be included in the canon because the male critics who control the classrooms and the critical conversation belong to a sphere of understanding separate from that of women authors:

The fictions that women compose about the worlds they inhabit may owe a debt to prior, influential works by other women or, simply enough, to the daily experience of the writer herself, or more usually, to some combination of the two. . . .

. . . The (usually male) reader who, both by experience and by reading, has never made acquaintance with those contexts—historically, the lying-in room, the parlor, the nursery, the kitchen, the laundry, and so on—will necessarily lack the capacity to fully interpret the dialogue or action embedded therein. (155)

By approaching women's texts with an eye for the nuances of women's culture and women's space, critics have been able to uncover greater complexities in women's writing; these complexities have become privileged by the academic community, suggesting that literary criticism can and does expand and alter its arena of concern. It is this capacity for change in study that we can exploit to further our understanding of ourselves and our culture.

With the door opened by the feminist critics of the 1970s and early 1980s, other critics have taken the study of women's writing in new directions. Josephine Donovan, for example, in her study of women's local color literature, identified a form of writing she called "woman- identified realism," which is not simply a critique of the male system and male writing but has goals and meanings of its own (1983, 3). The texts of writers such as Sarah Orne Jewett, Harriet Beecher Stowe, Rose Terry Cooke, Elizabeth Stuart Phelps, and Mary E. Wilkins Freeman reveal women's preoccupation with their own concerns, neither challenging nor avoiding the issues of male writers but rather creating a conversation among themselves and their readers. Judith Fetterley and Marjorie Pryse, in the introduction to their anthology *American Women Regionalists, 1850–1910*, similarly describe a collection of women writers who, consciously or not, created their own form of writing (1992); these authors—Stowe, Cooke, Jewett, Freeman, Kate Chopin, Alice Dunbar-Nelson, and Sui Sin Far, among others—all wrote from within a regional community, describing women's ways of defining themselves within specific historical and cultural contexts. Elizabeth Ammons argues that women's writing at the turn of the century is an important vehicle for looking at the relationship between gender and art (1992); writers such as Charlotte Perkins Gilman, Jewett, Chopin, Gertrude Stein, Sui Sin Far, Cather, Jessie Fauset, Wharton, and others, Ammons suggests, viewed writing as the creation of art, unlike their predecessors, who considered writing an occupation that brought in extra money. Ammons's goal "in pulling together turn-of-the-century women writers . . . to counteract the elitism that has allowed 'in' one or two of them—usually Wharton and Cather—thus divorcing them from other women writers, both of their generation and before them, and consigning those writers not plucked out to oblivion" (18) is an important part of feminist work in reexamining the literary canon and exposing its biases.

Most important, feminist critics have made clear the political implications of nineteenth-century women's writing. They have shown how events in "the lying-in room, the parlor, the nursery, the kitchen, the laundry" cannot be dismissed as trivial, private details. Jane Tompkins, for example, argues in *Sensational Designs* that nineteenth-century women's sentimental literature has been misunderstood by readers who fail to recognize the political implications of such writing: "[T]wentieth-century critics have taught generations of students to equate popularity with debasement, emotionality with ineffectiveness, religiosity with fakery, domesticity with triviality, and all of these, implicitly, with womanly inferiority" (1985, 123). Tompkins's work enables us to situate sentimental writing as having a significant public element: the power to effect political change. Sharon Harris, in the introduction to her edited collection *Redefining the Political Novel*, contends: "To exclude the family from the political, especially in studies of pre-twentieth-century America, is to deny that arena in which women have most experience and from which their knowledge of the need for change most often has been drawn" (1995, xiv). Harris calls for a reexamination of knowledge itself—of what counts as valued experience and of what experiences give an individual the authority to speak on public life.

Critics have helped readers understand domestic writing as a way for women to portray their inner lives and at the same time comment on the social and political contexts in which they live. In *The Home Plot: Women, Writing, and Domestic Ritual*, Ann Romines shows how domestic writing is a means for women to express themselves and to recount and refashion their experiences (1992). Domesticity, Romines maintains, was a way for women to exert control over their lives, especially with the absence of men in post–Civil War life. Housekeeping took on "godlike status" as a means of keeping back chaos—even if that status is illusory (10). Romines looks particularly at domestic ritual, events that are characterized by regular recurrence, symbolic meaning, emotional significance, and group bonding (12). The nineteenth-century local colorists passed down to their twentieth-century descendents a tool through which they could explore the implications of the changes in the outer world; Romines argues that Jewett's *Country of the Pointed Firs* (1896) broke ground by privileging material previously considered private. Jewett's earlier work,

Deephaven (1878), Romines shows, responds directly to social conditions: the increased tourism that caused New England city dwellers to travel to the country in the summer and the changing economy of Maine. As Romines explains, "the literary representation of domestic ritual allows writers to scrutinize their characters in the most social *and* the most inward and private of moments, which sometimes occur simultaneously" (14). Domestic writing is more than a private record of an individual woman's life in her home; it is the representation of the power dynamics and social inscriptions that structure the life of the home, for women and for men.

Helen Fiddyment Levy argues similarly in *Fiction of the Home Place* that nineteenth-century domestic writing was a means for women to show domestic life as a model for a democratic America (1992, 7). Female writers challenged the male use of and domination of the land—a patriarchal assertion of individual power (8)—while, she claims, women put forth an "ideal of moderation" (10) and emphasized the communal over the individualistic. Like Romines's work, Levy's study shows the political implications of women's domestic writing, in particular of women writers' engagement with nationality. Despite women's emphasis on the community as a socializing force instead of on the a priori existence of the individual, domestic writing in fact fulfills the requirements for "Americanness" that Baym discusses: Much domestic writing reveals tensions within American life. Thus late-nineteenth- and early-twentieth-century American domestic writing exposes the breakdown between the public and the private that would continue with the changes the First World War brought, and many women authors would continue to explore these changes through domestic writing.

Significantly, recognition of the political nature of everyday life is not limited to writing by women, as Lauren Berlant shows. In *The Anatomy of National Fantasy* (1991) she explores nineteenth-century daily life and nationality, focusing on Nathaniel Hawthorne's *Scarlet Letter*. She argues that "both the utopian and the practical operations of national existence hold daily life in hostage: and that daily life, in refracting the utopian and pragmatic strains of modern sociality, is the place where the historical uncanny and the future, unimaginable form somehow meet. . . . [T]he crisis of political identity is experienced, in [*The Scarlet Letter*], as a crisis of everyday life" (192). To study daily life and its political implications in novels by men is a natural extension of earlier work by feminist critics, and my project relies on this extension as a way to read men's novels about war.

Whereas domestic writing in the nineteenth century has received a fair amount of critical attention, domestic writing in the early part of the twentieth century has been overshadowed by the modernist literary movement.[1]

Modernist literature is commonly perceived as antisentimental and antido-mestic; the problems of literary classification can inscribe readers' reactions to texts. Suzanne Clark tackles this problem of antagonism between liter-ary forms in her book *Sentimental Modernisms*, arguing that modernism was based on a rejection of sentimental literature, which itself was inextricably associated with women (1991). For modernist women writers, writing cre-ated a conflict in the necessity of rejecting women's sentimental literary past. For women, Clark shows, this break meant the loss of a feminine her-itage and an alignment with a masculine tradition; for all writers and read-ers the "modernist exclusion of everything but the forms of high art acted like a machine for cultural loss of memory" (6).

The modernist movement is commonly understood to be a reaction against restrictive Victorian values made inapplicable by twentieth-century developments in technology, the introduction of the ideas of thinkers such as Freud and Darwin, and the devastation of the First World War—all developments that undermined previously unquestioned views about society and an individual's role in it. Modernism became a way to question social expectations, creating an attitude of disillusionment and skepticism. Until recently, critics identified as "modernist" those works in which criticism of society is overt, reflected in both style and content; T. S. Eliot, Ernest Hemingway, Gertrude Stein, F. Scott Fitzgerald, Ezra Pound, William Faulkner, John Dos Passos, Langston Hughes—these writers all directly challenge social norms.

Yet ideas about the home were also greatly affected by developments in technology, Darwinism, psychoanalytic theory, and World War I. Glenna Matthews, for example, points out that, in the post-Freudian family, women were expected to take as much "responsibility for the emotional well-being of the society as ever" yet were seen to have "a diminished capacity to meet that responsibility" (1987, 181). Mothers were under-stood to be the center of psychological development—and not in a good way; they became ever at fault for the traumas inflicted on the child. Furthermore, Matthews points out that technological advances, such as the introduction of the automobile, displaced mothers from the spiritual center of the home to its service center; the "soccer mom" role may seem to have evolved with the introduction of the minivan, but in fact even in the 1920s women were expected to be the family chauffeur (192). Women's domestic writing reflects both these changes in society and the pressures they placed on women and on the home.

Romines's and Levy's studies of domestic writing in the twentieth cen-tury (both critics look at authors such as Ellen Glasgow, Willa Cather, and Eudora Welty, for example) help us understand that modernism did not mean the disappearance of domestic writing. Rather, some women writers addressed changes in thought brought about by the war, industrialization, immigration, Freud, and Darwin—to name only a few—in works about the home and domestic ritual. These works challenge the limits of "woman's sphere" as well as the definition of "domestic novel."

For this project, as in Romines's *Home Plot* (1992), the term "domestic novel" refers to novels that rely on the events and quiet rituals of everyday life as part of the text's system of meaning. These novels focus on primarily private matters yet reveal much about the characters' broader social and political contexts. Dynamics of power, value, and meaning can be interpreted by reading closely details about food, housing, and personal relationships. Yet I also look at war writing by men; even though I do not consider these works domestic novels, I do believe that the role of domestic detail and domestic ritual in these works is as significant as it is in much writing by women.

Unlike the domestic novel, the war novel appears to have a fairly stable and consistent literary history. Most war novels are about men who go to battle, often undergoing a profound psychological change throughout the course of the novel and the fighting. In *American War Literature 1914 to Vietnam* Jeffrey Walsh describes the plot of a typical U.S. war novel as a young soldier's idealistically going to war; mixing with men from all classes, races, and backgrounds; coming to disillusionment with the older culture that caused the war; and giving rise to a new, youthful culture (1982, 5). For U.S. soldiers who participated in the First World War, Stephen Crane's Civil War novel, *The Red Badge of Courage*, was particularly influential (1895). Stanley Cooperman, in his classic *World War I and the American Novel*, describes Crane's work as glorifying war as "the magnificent proving ground, an area where cause is internal rather than external, affected by individual will rather than by political, economic, or (perhaps most important in terms of World War I combat experience) technological determinism" (1967, 47). But World War I was fought differently from the way the Civil War was—no hand-to-hand combat, no direct engagement, no glory to be won by personal valor, only impersonal death by shells fired by an enemy one rarely saw. U.S. soldiers with only the Civil War as a model were unprepared for the type of warfare and the type of experience they would endure. The American expectation about war as a proving ground was shown to be false; instead the soldier found himself important only insofar as he was part of a mass (88). Cooperman argues that in fact Crane was integral to the disillusionment U.S. soldiers experienced: "Correctly estimating the influence of Crane, students of war literature have tended to underestimate the enormous contrast between the symbolic combat experience he described (war as the achievement of manhood) and the actual experience of World War I—a contrast rendered all the more psychologically and emotionally damaging precisely because of Crane's influence" (47). Thus American literary responses to the First World War show disillusionment with the society that caused the war and that represented war through a literary heritage that failed them utterly.

Cooperman, like Walsh, suggests that to be a war novel a text must show the disillusionment of the soldier with the world of ideals—a world represented not only by Crane but also, and perhaps more important, by women. Cooperman argues that sentimental war literature, widely read before and during the First World War and "usually [written] by lady authors such as Mary Raymond Shipman Andrews, Temple Bailey, or (unfortunately) Edith Wharton" (19), "must be understood clearly—perhaps even harshly—if we are to understand the mental framework of disgust and mockery from which young writers created their testaments of disillusion" (33). This definition of a war novel, then, inherently necessitates a rejection of women's writing, and this rejection is perpetrated by both male authors and critics who have consistently addressed male writers as authorities on war even as they belittle women's works that deal with war. Yet, as Baym comments on American women's writing, a greater understanding of women's texts unsettles this definition (1985). Willa Cather's One of Ours (1922), for example, is both a domestic novel and a war novel, and it also, like more canonical World War I novels, suggests a dissatisfaction with the world of ideals.

In fact, a closer look at American men's writing about war suggests their fundamental debt to writing by nineteenth-century women novelists. Evelyn Cobley's Representing War: Form and Ideology in First World War Narratives (1993) approaches World War I novels as an examination of form, and she points to a very real problem for the writers of such narratives: "the realization that the narrative had to be addressed either to those who already knew and did not need to be told or to those who did not know and could never be made to understand" (7). The difficulty, Cobley argues, is that writing about the First World War is an impossible task to begin with; the war defied everything the soldiers knew about war, but they had no way to express their experiences except through literary forms already established, forms that "reproduce . . . the ideological values against which they are being mobilized" (10). Thus works that other critics read as antiwar and antiestablishment Cobley sees as unable to resist the ideological structures that brought about the war in the first place. Thomas Boyd's Through the Wheat (1923), for example, relies on details of everyday life to describe the experience of war; intending to challenge the ideological assumptions of his readers by recounting horrors so minutely, Boyd instead reverts to a system of knowledge that underlies the Western tradition. Soldier-writers of the First World War, Cobley suggests, are bound by systems of meaning that carry over from the nineteenth century into the twentieth century; that is, their work is embedded in what Cobley calls "the Enlightenment project of infinite social progress through rational organization" (1993, 4). As Cobley argues, "[w]hat the urge to name and classify in war narratives indicates is less a need to master the unnameable chaos of front-line experience than a desire to contain a threat to Enlightenment confidence in ideals epitomized in the scientific method and the power of reason" (56–57).

This system of knowledge is directly connected to women's domestic writing. In domestic novels, as Romines argues, details of daily life are offered as testimony to a woman's social, political, and cultural roles (1992); similarly, in war novels, writers provide catalogs of details to prove the truth and legitimacy of their experiences. As Cobley argues, "[a]lthough the war narratives repeatedly proclaimed that the war defied human understanding, their descriptive method privileges a modernist mentality which sought to control both the natural and the social world by collapsing reality into what is *classifiable*" (1993, 56). To advance our understanding of the relationship between the war novel and the domestic novel, we must understand that women domestic writers and male war writers use the same strategy to express their world.

When discussing the American World War I novel, critics refer primarily to works by Ernest Hemingway, John Dos Passos, and other male writers who "were there." In more recent years, however, feminist critics have begun to challenge the notion of what a war novel is by redefining who could write one; that is, critics have noted women's participation in World War I as nurses, reporters, volunteers, ambulance drivers, supply clerks, and observers and acknowledged that all of these roles have given women a legitimate viewpoint from which to write. Critics such as Claire Tylee, Dorothy Goldman, Helen Cooper, and Margaret Randolph Higonnet all discuss the ways in which women participated in the First World War as well as the ways their writing responded to the war. Furthermore, Nicola Beauman shows how the events and attitudes of the war carried over in British consciousness and British literature long after the war itself ended; she points out, referring to British writers, that "[e]ven if a woman novelist is not overtly a 'war' novelist, and even if her work lacks references to the War . . . , it is in fact a rare novel that does not refer to the War in some way" (1993, 129). The critics listed earlier, however, address primarily the work of British women writers, such as Virginia Woolf, May Sinclair, or Evadne Price, or of American expatriate women writers such as Edith Wharton, Gertrude Stein, and Mildred Aldrich. Willa Cather, with her Pulitzer-prize-winning novel *One of Ours*, tends to be the notable exception.

My present study fills a significant gap: I look at the writing of American women about the First World War in interdependent relation to the writing of American men. These women writers—Temple Bailey, Ellen Glasgow, Willa Cather, Edith Wharton, and Eudora Welty—use domestic language as a medium for commenting on the larger, seemingly more public, sphere of war. Beauman's comment applies to American women's writing as well; not only were women writers influenced by the beginning and the actual event of World War I, they continued to feel and write about its impact after it was over. At the same time I expand Kolodny's methods for rereading to look at the domestic details that appear in men's texts—in this case, men's war novels. Male writers may not have had extensive experience with the kitchen, the laundry, and the lying-in room, but certainly they were aware of the domestic ritual that Romines describes and in which they themselves played a role. War novels often portray male soldiers reproducing the domestic world on their own.

I am not the first to engage in a feminist revision of literary genres, of course, and the critics before me have shown ways in which one might approach such a study. Just as Clark challenges the separation of the masculine modernist and feminine sentimental traditions, Elizabeth Jane Harrison's *Female Pastoral: Women Writers Re-Visioning the American South* shows that the division of literary categories often occurs through assumptions about gender (1991). She argues that although the pastoral tradition has usually been perceived as male, in fact women writers such as Ellen Glasgow, Margaret Mitchell, Willa Cather, and Alice Walker have appropriated the genre to challenge the male pastoral genre and to make their own statements about gender, community, and land. Elizabeth Abel, Marianne Hirsch, and Elizabeth Langland's edited collection *The Voyage In: Fictions of Female Development* (1983) and Rachel Blau DuPlessis's *Writing beyond the Ending: Narrative Strategies of Twentieth-Century Women Writers* (1985) explore the implications of the *bildungsroman* structure and plot for women and women writers; both studies show that such a plot requires creative and unique responses from women.

Yet, as well as demonstrating that women writers responded to the war novel through particularly feminine strategies, I also suggest that men writers responded to the domestic novel by incorporating its techniques into their writing. Just as ideas of home and war influence each other, so writing about the home and writing about war influence each other—a battle, as Sandra Gilbert and Susan Gubar argue in *No Man's Land: The War of the Words* (1988), but also a system of literary interdependence.

Acknowledgments

This project is the culmination of many people's labor and time, and I owe them a debt of gratitude. I would like to thank Linda Wagner-Martin for her guidance and advice and without whom this book would never have been written. Thanks are also due to Kathleen Drowne, Kelly Reames, Scott Walker, Shannon Wooden, and Lara Kees for their comments on the manuscript and for their ongoing moral support. I must also thank Ethan Lewis for his thoughtful contributions and Nancy Perkins for pushing me across the finish line.

Thanks to the Willa Cather Symposium, the Ellen Glasgow Society, the Modern Language Association, the Mid-Atlantic Popular Culture/American Culture Association, and the Southern Writers Symposium, at which parts of this project were first presented, and to *The Hemingway Review*, in which a version of chapter 4 was first published in Spring 2000.

Introduction
American Domesticity and the
First World War

In Louisa May Alcott's *Little Women* (1868–69), a novel usually considered entrenched in the domestic literary tradition, Mr. March, a chaplain in the Union army, writes to his daughters that he knows they "will do their duty faithfully, fight their bosom enemies bravely, and conquer themselves so beautifully that when I come back to them I may be fonder and prouder than ever of my little women." The March girls learn to control their vanity and their desires for little pleasures because of the ever-present thought of their father and other men suffering in battle and in the cold. Jo thinks that "keeping her temper at home was a much harder task than facing a rebel or two down South" (10). Womanhood in Alcott's novel is defined through response to the absent yet central event of the Civil War. In this way, *Little Women* can be read as a war novel—a novel about the Civil War as experienced on the home front.

Fewer than twenty-five years later, Stephen Crane published *The Red Badge of Courage* (1895), a story that has become a classic American tale of men's experience in war. Even though the novel describes young Henry Fleming's growth to adulthood amidst the violence and chaos of the Civil War, the text depends on the inclusion of domestic references to illustrate the event of war: "[Henry] had had the belief that real war was a series of death struggles with small time in between for sleep and meals; but since his regiment had come to the field the army had done little but sit still and try to keep warm" (Crane 1951, 11). Instead of a long, continuous experience of violence, Henry finds, war is a repetition of incidents at home but in a harsher environment. When they finally begin to move, the troops rid themselves of all equipment except guns and food: "You can now eat and shoot. . . . That's all you want to do," one soldier tells another (33). Such details included with the fighting and with Henry's private battles give a picture of war; fighting, the obvious activity of war, becomes immediately linked to eating, an activity usually associated with home and ritual. As a war novel, Crane's work became an important vehicle by which soldiers approached the First World War. Taken together, *The Red Badge of Courage* and *Little Women* are important precursors to understanding literature—both women's and men's—about the First World War and critical responses to that literature.

This project examines two categories of novels: domestic writing and war writing, both set around the time of World War I. "Domestic writing" here is a concept inherited from nineteenth-century women writers and describes works that depict women and families in their homes and that use household rituals as a way to express meaning, both about women's private lives and about their larger social context. "War writing" refers to works, usually (but not always) by men, about the experience of a man going to war and suffering disillusionment with society as a result of his war experiences. Bringing these categories together furthers our comprehension of the American sense of self during this time—how men and women understood themselves in terms of gender, violence, and tradition. Separating these categories into distinct and unyielding classifications blocks our view of what literature does. If we can see how domestic novels treat the war, we can gain insight into how war novels treat the war and the home.

My selection of novels about World War I differs significantly from the list many critics would draw up. My aim is not to prove that women were involved in the First World War and responded to it through their writing, a task already ably under way by collections such as Margaret R. Higonnet et al's *Behind the Lines: Gender and the Two World Wars* (1987) and Helen M. Cooper, Adrienne Auslander Munich, and Susan Merrill Squier's *Arms and the Woman: War, Gender, and Literary Representation* (1989). Instead, my intention is to explore the relationship between writing about war and writing about the home in a specifically American context; to do so I have chosen to look at traditional war novels such as Ernest Hemingway's *Farewell to Arms* (1929) as well as domestic novels such as Eudora Welty's *Delta Wedding* (1946) that do not immediately present themselves as being about war. My purpose in such a reading is to explore connections between kinds of writing that have been separated by literary definitions. This separation is founded on false premises: that women's experience of themselves in the home is isolated from politics and war and that men's writing about war is not directly influenced by women's writing. In fact, similar cultural and political impulses affect both kinds of writing.

Although many studies address British and American World War I literature together, here I isolate texts written by Americans for two reasons.[1] First, the United States' participation in the war was gradual, as people debated for years over the meaning of the war in Europe and its relationship to Americans and American values. U.S. soldiers' experience in the war occurred over a much shorter period of time than did that of European soldiers; the United States was officially in the war for about eighteen months, with soldiers actually in Europe for approximately half that time. Second, as discussed in the preface, by the First World War Americans had their own distinct literary heritage, and writing produced from the war reflected that heritage, although I do not mean to suggest that British and European influences were nonexistent. But, as Stanley Cooperman argues about the significance of Crane's *Red Badge of Courage*, soldiers from the United States brought with them different pre-conceived notions of what war would be like based on literature that had captured their imaginations (1967). In addition, soldiers' attitudes toward the war were greatly influenced by their attitudes toward the home, a home that created in them their sense of patriotism and idealism and that was distinctly American.

By viewing writing about the home and writing about war in light of each other, we see that war and domestic life exist on a continuum. The ideology that defines domesticity rests on gender roles, roles that define who goes to war and who stays at home. Domestic novels reflected and shaped an American mindset that prepared soldiers for war and defined women's response to their men. Temple Bailey's *Tin Soldier* (1918), for example, depicts an ideology of war that romanticizes the battle experience, equates women's home-front work with men's war-front work, and makes the possibility of both men and women fulfilling their roles dependent on each other's success at their work. Soldiers came to understand the field of battle through their understanding of the home—and they understood the home in light of what they learned in war. Literary soldiers such as Cather's Claude Wheeler and John Dos Passos's Martin Howe come to distrust the home because it is implicated so profoundly in war propaganda. Domestic and war novels converse with each other about important topics such as gender, violence, death, nationality, and morality.

The structure of domestic and war experiences is in many ways remark-ably similar: Both are marked by a need for order in a chaotic world as well as a feeling that small rituals can create a place of safety. If the housekeeper cleans, as Ann Romines suggests, to keep nature under control and to gain a sense of power within her confined life, the soldier sets up his own rituals to keep the random forces of death at bay. Both kinds of writing address the idea of the individual within a larger unit, either the family or the military; both describe strategies through which individuals seek to survive and to be remembered within the unit. Eric J. Leed, in writing about the rituals and liminality of the First World War, suggests that com-paring war experiences to rituals of passage "allows us to set aside for a moment the notion that war is solely aggression and violence, and it also permits us to see the conventional nature of those discontinuities between life in times of peace and war" (1979, 13). That is, viewing war as ritual reveals the constructed nature of daily experience even in "normal" times. Nancy Huston, in her essay "The Matrix of War: Mothers and Heroes," examines mythical and historical archetypes to explain the almost universal linkage between motherhood and soldiering; she shows how the language of one becomes the language of the other—of war as a birthing process, of birthing as a battle (1986, 133–34). The male sphere of war and the female sphere of home are literally and mythically experienced as parallel structures.

Thus literary representations about home and war rely on similar strategies and perhaps also face similar difficulties. Historian David M. Kennedy argues that the writing of most soldiers about the war—diaries, journals, and letters—reads like travel writing or propaganda. Because the average U.S. soldier saw battle only briefly, most soldiers' writings address "the quaint antiquity of this town, or that church or chateau, their imaginations especially fired by the evocation of names from the history books" (1980, 206). They wrote about French people, places, and customs, especially rituals and religion (208–9), and they also commented on army conditions: "In vivid contrast with the wooden descriptions of tourist sights are the lively and lavish descriptions of those rare meals eaten somewhere—anywhere—other than the military mess. The careful recording of menus, indeed, took up a great deal of space in many soldiers' diaries and letters" (209). Michael Reynolds, in *Hemingway's First War*, points out that by including such precise details in *A Farewell to Arms* about streets, hotels, and cafes, Hemingway writes about Italy like a travel guide (1976, 223). In *Representing War*, Evelyn Cobley addresses the ideological effect such a writing style has on our understanding of the First World War. Soldier-writers worried about writing that distorted their experiences and so felt a need to rely on descriptions of "everyday events" (1993, 6) to carry their narratives—a problematic technique for writers attempting to describe unprecedented experiences, as Cobley shows, yet a significant point when considering the relationship between men's writing about war and women's writing about the home. This strategy of writing the everydayness as well as describing French scenery and customs can be traced back to nineteenth-century travel and local color writing, much of it written by women.

Romines points out that the literary category "local color" has been problematic for women writers because it becomes "a conveniently parenthetical territory in which to colonize the successful American women writers who were contemporaries of James and Howells" (1992, 28). Romines isolates domesticity as the source of confusion in categorizing women writers as local colorists, realists, or sentimentalists. As a way to work out of this muddle, she uses domestic ritual as a critical tool: "*Ritual* implies repetition because the repeated act has or creates meaning, which becomes tradition through its continuance. *Domestic* implies an enclosure, somehow sacralized, which is both the house and the perceiving self" (29). If women's writing can be "rescued" from the ghetto of "local color" through the perception of domestic ritual, domestic ritual can also be used to help make sense—a different sense, perhaps, than is usually brought out of such works—of men's war writing.

The First World War was at its root, many people believed, a war about the preservation of civilization. At the time, the war was represented as a crusade necessary to preserve Western culture; one propaganda poster produced in the United States shows an apelike creature with a club labeled "*kultur*" in one arm and a ravished woman in the other threatening the United States. Edith Wharton's George Campton, in A *Son at the Front* (1923), first approaches the war with the feeling that "the whole affair, from the point of view of twentieth-century civilization, was too monstrous an incongruity for something not to put a stop to it at the eleventh hour" (32). Using a progressive model of civilization, George believes that violence and aggression such as the Germans are exhibiting indicate a regression to an earlier state. When news comes that Germany has in fact invaded Belgium, George feels that a civilized society has a moral imperative to stop such savagery: "The howling blackguards! The brigands! This isn't war—it's simple murder!" (90). Indeed, with the United States protected from the European conflict by an ocean, the question of whether to enter the war was more an ideological issue than one of physical threat. Even literary criticism of World War I literature tends to focus on the ideals for which men fought and the soldiers' profound disillusionment, a disillusionment that in some ways sparked the modernist movement and that marked literature, the arts, and our image of post–World War I society, especially the "lost generation."

This approach, then, is partly an attempt to conduct a literary criticism that takes into account those things that define civilization. Certainly things such as education, literacy, and the arts are significant, but "civilized" societies are ritualized at the most basic levels. Food, shelter, clothing—we take them for granted; yet the way we treat them is part of what makes us define ourselves as civilized. And so reading the significance of the domestic details in war novels can be as productive as reading such details in domestic novels. When a female writer describes a woman baking a cake, we can read in her actions the personal and cultural significance of cake baking; the ritual surrounding the activity and subsequently around the consumption of the cake tells us much about that society's values, hierarchies, and subtleties. When a soldier uses his bayonet to pry open a can of meat that looks like rotting flesh, we see both a distortion of "civilized" rituals and the creation of new ones. Who eats what, who cooks what, who sleeps where, who wears what clothing—all of these basic details tell us much, as anthropologists know. When a writer includes or leaves out these and a myriad of other details, we are given clues about a character's values, beliefs, sense of self, and sense of community.

Whereas the domestic world is occupied by two sexes, however, the military world is inhabited, historically, by only one, and the presence of the domestic within the war novel is not without tension. In the military, by necessity men (both actual and literary) take on traditionally female roles such as cooking and nursing and even homemaking—the imbuing of a space with emotional significance. Thus soldiers' relationship to gender becomes redefined; oddly, this new relationship tends to reflect a greater comfort with filling feminine roles than one might expect. This comfort may grow out of soldiers' need to distance themselves from the home front for which they are fighting. Sometimes soldiers, such as Cather's Claude Wheeler, have gone to the war precisely to create that distance. But the idea of home still maintains its appeal; in *No Man's Land* Leed explains how the World War I soldier became separated from home and at the same time tried to re-create a sense of home at the front—an attempt ever futile, as men died and were continually replaced, preventing the sense of security that the idea of home inherently provides (1979, 210). Literary responses to war thus reflect both an antagonism toward and a longing for the domestic world. In Hemingway's *Farewell to Arms*, for example, Frederic Henry both longs for and resents the homey comforts Catherine Barkley offers and represents. The domestic becomes a source of origin, an object of desire, and a point of rebellion.

Although this project explores domesticity and domestic ritual in novels by women and men, it also provides a way of looking at violence, particularly at the ways in which American domestic culture around the time of World War I reinforced and incorporated sanctioned violence. Jean Bethke Elshtain's concept of the paired "Beautiful Soul" and the "Just Warrior" explains the interdependence of female and male roles in creating an ideology that permitted the violence of war while maintaining the sanctity of the home (1987). Huston describes a mythical and literary relationship between war and childbearing; men go to war, she argues, because women have children (1986). Elshtain's and Huston's works provide a framework for my argument. I show how, at the beginning of the twentieth century, the ideology of domesticity was already prepared to allow for the idea of war and to send men to battle.

When World War I began, the burgeoning and reasonably successful suffrage movement and other progressive reform efforts were threatened by a need for national unity. Women's issues were pushed aside for war, which was perceived as the greater cause. Though some women's groups agitated for peace, other women chose to speak out in favor of the war, if only to prevent losing political ground. The role of women and that of women writers were being challenged in different ways; as Gilbert and Gubar argue in Volume 1 of *No Man's Land: The War of the Words*, the early twentieth century saw a pitched battle between male and female writers over the right to describe and define the literary terrain (1988). Women's participation in the sexual battle—whether in the political, social, or literary arena—partly assumed the shape of asserting the right to talk about war. And women's writing about war was often closely related, even integral, to their writing about the home. Propaganda for the war, for example, created a sense of women's duty to support their men and to send their husbands and sons to battle, and women writers had to decide how they would respond to such propaganda and consequently how they would place themselves and their work in respect to the national ideology.

Even though women and the home figured prominently in propaganda for the war, the home failed dismally to prepare soldiers for what they would experience. War ideology suggested that men would go forth and fight for the honor of their women and country, as Dos Passos's Dan Fuselli pictures himself "shooting dozens of men in green uniforms, and he thought of Mabe reading about it in the papers" (1997, 39). Yet mechanized warfare, in which soldiers were sitting targets, forced to remain still, frozen in the mud of the trenches, was a sharp disjunction from the valorized warfare through which men and women imagined the war and through which American culture defined gender. For soldiers, disillusionment about war was often accompanied by a deep resentment of women and, by extension, U.S. society. In Dos Passos's *One Man's Initiation*, a soldier scorns "Hun-hatin' women, if they're male or female" (1969, 73). After the war, the American home was unprepared to receive back its soldiers. Whereas the men had experienced disillusionment with the ideals of war, people at home knew little about its actualities. The more subtle principles of violence on which the home operated did not correspond to the violence the men faced. The structure of the American family itself became unsettled, a testing ground for a changing dynamic between men and women.

The first chapter explores the relationship between the ideology of war and the ideology of the home in the prewar United States in novels written by women. In her propagandistic novel *The Tin Soldier* (1918), Temple Bailey addresses these questions: What role does the United States have in the war, and how can the individual fulfill his or her responsibilities to a nation at war? This novel shows how directly the ideology of war depends on the ideology of the home, for the hero can go to war only if his wife is able to maintain the home in his absence; one cannot function without the other. Ellen Glasgow too sought to understand the reasons for and implications of the First World War, particularly how gender roles shape war ideology. In *The Builders* (1919), the world of the home becomes a microcosm for the issues the nation at large was facing. Later, women writers looked back on prewar America and questioned the ideological underpinnings of the war. Glasgow's *Sheltered Life* (1932) and Willa Cather's *One of Ours* (1922) show the changing ideological stances in America leading to the country's participation in World War I, and these novels question the cultural implications of such ideologies.

The second chapter discusses the intricate relationships between parents and their soldier sons. The ideology of war demands a dependent relationship between men and women; this relationship takes on different aspects when the men and women are sons and mothers. A short propaganda piece, Grace Richmond's *Whistling Mother* (1917), provides an idea of popular conceptions of the mother of a soldier, and Freud's ideas about family relationships are useful for understanding the power dynamics among mothers, fathers, and sons. Cather and Edith Wharton challenge Richmond's easy stereotypes and explore the complexities of the relationships between parents and soldiers. In *One of Ours*, Claude Wheeler's relationship with his mother suggests Oedipal impulses that relate directly to the causes of the war (Cather 1922). Similarly, Wharton's *Son at the Front* (1923) implies that incestuous feelings of a father for his son undermine the principles on which the Allies claim to be fighting and establishes the gulf that war experience exacerbates in the relationship of two people—a gulf that Western civilization makes inherent in personal relationships.

The third chapter examines the last part of *One of Ours* and several other traditional war novels written by men: Thomas Boyd's *Through the Wheat* (1923) and John Dos Passos's *One Man's Initiation: 1917* (1920) and *Three Soldiers* (1921). While these novels show the devastation the First World War perpetrated on the soldier's sense of himself, attention to domestic details in these works reveals the need for domestic ritual as a way to resist such a destruction of self. In addition, reading these war novels in light of the domestic tradition shows the writers' attempts to react against the society that created such a horror of a war.

The fourth chapter focuses specifically on the World War I writing of Ernest Hemingway. *In Our Time* (1925) and *A Farewell to Arms* (1929) show a longing for the security of domesticity and an attempt to reconcile the violence of war with childbearing. The framework that Huston proposed in "The Matrix of War" provides further insight into Hemingway's ambivalent conceptions of both war and gender (1986). His writings about the war include women to a much larger extent than do works by other male authors, and because of the presence of women we can see how his male characters rely on and understand the importance of domestic ritual for emotional security.

The fifth chapter explores the relationship of war and domestic writing in terms of the implications the First World War had for the future of the United States. William Faulkner's first novel, *Soldiers' Pay* (1926), describes soldiers' return and their attempts to integrate themselves into domestic life. In particular, the novel explores the new relationships between men and women and reevaluates the domestic ideology emphasized before the war. An examination of Eudora Welty's *Delta Wedding* (1945) further expands the issues Huston raises—that is, the relationship between men's war making and women's childbearing. After the war, the dead Denis Fairchild, as well as other Fairchild soldiers, become part of the family structure of women mourning their men. Ellen Fairchild risks her life on her tenth pregnancy while her brother-in-law, a veteran of World War I, searches for love in an "unsuitable" marriage.

This study makes connections to show the instability of the differences we rely on critically. This kind of reading takes into account the things not seen, although they are there: domestic rituals present in texts by both women and men. That these texts are about war makes such details even more significant, for the experience of war is a culturally created one, as is the experience of home. Looking at these texts together shows us not only that the gulf between men's and women's writing and between men's and women's lives is culturally created but also that we can cross that gulf.

Chapter 1
The Ideology of Domesticity and War in World War I

The ideologies both of home and of war depend on, even demand, the establishment of specific gender roles. Women, historically, have tended the home and family; in the nineteenth century in particular women became the repository for ideals such as beauty, love, and religion. Barbara Welter argues that as American men made their way in the increasingly industrialized world, women were expected to protect the values that society thought men could no longer hold without help (1976). Carroll Smith-Rosenberg, for example, describes middle-class, nineteenth-century America as a world with two very different and very distinct spheres (1985). The ideals of this division carried over into twentieth-century American literature and were particularly prominent in women's texts about the First World War.

War, as it has historically been constructed and experienced, divides people according to sex, sending the men out to battle while the women remain at home. This division justifies itself even as it occurs: Women stay at home because only men can fight, and only men can fight because they must protect the women at home. In *Women and War* (1987), Jean Bethke Elshtain explains the nature of these roles; she points out that Western tradition dictates that "in times of war, real men and women—locked in a dense symbiosis, perceived as beings who have complementary needs and exemplifying gender-specific virtues—take on, in cultural memory and narrative, the personas of Just Warriors and Beautiful Souls" (4). The Beautiful Soul is a Hegelian concept that Bethke applies to Western women as a group: "[T]he female Beautiful Soul in time of war has been positioned as a mourner, an occasion for war, and a keeper of the flame of nonwarlike values" (144). It is important to note that although the Beautiful Soul is associated with "nonwarlike values," she nevertheless "exhort[s] men to their task, sustain[s] their efforts, honor[s] their deeds, mourn[s] their loss" (149). She is an ideal of peace and love that participates in the construct of war. This "dense symbiosis" of gender and the similarities between the ideologies of home and war indicate that they

1

are in fact one ideology—an idea that invites closer examination. How do ideas about war influence ideas about the home? How does what occurs in the home affect attitudes—both men's and women's—about war?

Before and during the First World War, propaganda—both visual and print—defined these roles and the dynamic between war and domesticity. In her study *Imaging American Women* (1987), Martha Banta explores the ways in which women have been popularly portrayed in the United States, and in particular she argues that

> When 1917 came the United States was ready for a poster war. The government fumbled its way into the tardy training and equipping of troops for overseas combat, but signboards and marketing devices were already at hand. Advertising agencies had created experts at the sale of goods to American consumers by means of emotional appeals that stimulated desire. With the inception of the war effort, the same men were ready to sell Americans a new set of desires based on the notion of service to the nation. . . . What remained a constant was their calculated incorporation of female figures as vehicles for the simplified representation of a complex of values. (578–79)

Banta demonstrates that the history of women on such posters comprises two types of women, the Amazon Warrior and the Protecting Angel, and it is during World War I, she argues, that these two images of women converge (562–64), indicating the emergence of a new ideal: woman as an equal in war through her powers of healing and protection. The use of images of women on World War I posters was intended to evoke specific responses, namely a sense of patriotism and self-sacrifice from both men and women and a reinforcement of gender roles. Domestic novels written by women both reflected and questioned those roles. Although Elshtain emphasizes that the Beautiful Soul and the Just Warrior are never actually real people, they in fact appear as characters in propaganda and literature. Part of the purpose of this chapter is to demonstrate how women's literature about World War I relied on and interrogated women's role as Elshtain's Beautiful Souls and Banta's Warrior/Angel and why such a dynamic between men and women was necessary.

Unlike nations such as Britain and France, the United States had no obvious investment in the First World War, and Americans, who had not been interested in European affairs for many decades, were reluctant to abandon their isolationist stance for a cause apparently unconnected to American life. As David Kennedy points out, the people of the United States were facing problems such as conflicts between labor and management; the assimilation of new immigrants; and pressure from a wave of reformers for social and political change (1980, 11). The pacifist movement was strongly entrenched; sixty-seven-year-old Senator Henry Cabot Lodge even got into a fistfight with one peace activist in the Capitol building. In addition, President Woodrow Wilson was well aware that the demands accompanying his request for a declaration of war—"his proposals for heavy taxation, for universal military training, for the repression of supposed disloyalty, and for the paramountcy of the Executive in wartime" (15)—would in themselves be controversial. The war, and U.S. participation in it, required Americans to rethink how they saw themselves as a nation.

Although the United States assumed a position of neutrality during the first years of the war, government officials and other leaders were pro-Ally almost from the start of the conflict. The sinking of the *Lusitania* with the deaths of 128 Americans in May 1915 turned the country against Germany. Furthermore, the British had been subtly controlling media coverage of the war since its beginning. On the day they declared war on Germany, Britain cut the underwater cable lines from Germany to the United States; as a result, most of the information about the war that appeared in American publications came from British sources. In *Propaganda for War: How the United States Was Conditioned to Fight the Great War of 1914–1918* (1996), Stewart Halsey Ross shows that British propagandists were active within the United States for years before America declared war on Germany. One particularly important piece of propaganda, the *Report of the Committee on Alleged German Atrocities*, was produced by a British committee headed by Viscount James Bryce, a man highly respected for his scholarship. The Bryce Report, released in London and Washington on May 13, 1915, details horrors committed by the Germans, usually crimes against women and children:

> In Hofstade: Two young women were lying in the back yard of the house. One had her breasts cut off, the other had been attacked. . . .
> In Eldwyt: A man's naked body was tied up to a ring in the wall in the back yard of a house. He was dead, and his corpse was mutilated in a manner too horrible to record.
> In Boort Meerbaek: A German soldier was seen to fire three times at a little girl of five years old. Having failed to hit her, he subsequently bayonetted her. (quoted in Ross 1996, 54)

Ross points out that almost immediately after the war most if not all of the atrocities in the Bryce Report were proven to be false (24), yet at the time the stories, as they were meant to, inspired a sense of chivalry in the United States, a chivalry that was to be fundamental in shaping the popular view of the war. In contrast, Germany's efforts to win the United States to its side were clumsy and ineffectual, and the country did itself no favors by executing the British nurse Edith Cavell on October 12, 1915. Cavell, working in German-occupied Belgium, was herself committing war crimes by secretly shipping wounded British soldiers back to England, but "her violent death was every propagandist's dream come true" (70).

Thus from the beginning the war was presented to Americans in gendered terms and within a specifically heterosexual dynamic. Belgium as a country was pictured as a raped woman, and Belgian citizens were themselves shown as feminized and attacked. One U.S. propaganda poster, bearing the slogan "Remember Belgium," shows, against a background of flames, the dark outlines of a German soldier pulling along a resisting young girl. The United States was to be the masculine hero for the invaded, feminized Belgium. Such a gendered political landscape had important implications for gender dynamics on the home front. Men and women, like the representations of United States and Belgium, were characterized by gender stereotypes, and yet American women were called to service, as I show in this chapter, on the same terms as men, even if the service they were asked to perform was itself distinctly gendered. Women, then, became situated in an oddly self-reflexive position: They were in the feminized position of the victims, seen as representatives of what the men fought for, and at the same time they were asked to fight the war in a specifically feminine way.

Once the United States declared war in 1917, an American propaganda machine was put into place. After the war George Creel, the head of the Committee on Public Information, published his (somewhat glorified) account of the committee's activities in *How We Advertised America: The First Telling of the Amazing Story of the Committee on Public Information That Carried the Gospel of Americanism to Every Corner of the Globe* (1920). He backs his title with an even grander statement of the committee's impact:

> The trial of strength was not only between massed bodies of armed men, but between opposed ideals, and moral verdicts took on all the value of military decisions. Other wars went no deeper than the physical aspects, but German *Kultur* raised issues that had to be fought out in the hearts and minds of people as well as on the actual firing-line. The approval of the world meant the steady flow of inspiration into the trenches; it meant the strengthened resolve and the renewed determination of the civilian population that is a nation's second line. (3)

Figure 1. "Remember Belgium."
Photograph courtesy of the National Archives (4-P-2)

Despite the grandiose language and the implied fallacy that previous wars were not ideological, Creel's claims for importance were not unfounded. The First World War required U.S. mobilization on a scale never before attempted,[1] which in turn demanded an ideological and emotional commitment from American citizens—especially since there was no immediate physical threat to Americans. Propagandists did, however, suggest the

Figure 2. "Sow the Seeds." Photograph courtesy of the National Archives (4-P-59)

danger that the murdering, raping, and pillaging Germans could cross to the United States; one poster shows an ape, representing Germany, climbing onto American shores. The text reads: "Destroy this Mad Brute: If this War is not fought to a finish in Europe, it will be on the soil of the United States." Both Creel and this poster suggest an ideological battle—a struggle for cultural values—that was manifested in physical battle.

This struggle came directly into people's homes, especially their kitchens, as food restrictions were implemented as a way to support a U.S. army overseas.[2] The slogan "Can Vegetables, Fruit and the Kaiser too" (Ross 1996, 251) integrated the war into housekeeping. As the controllers of food, women were targeted as an especially important part of the war effort through special poster propaganda campaigns. One poster, put out by the U.S. Food Administration, enjoins viewers to "Be Patriotic: sign your country's pledge to save the food." Another shows a woman draped in the U.S. flag planting seeds, with the slogan: "Sow the seeds of Victory! Plant & raise your own vegetables." At the bottom is the phrase "Every Garden a Munition Plant" along with directions for writing to the National War Garden Commission for instructions on "gardening, canning, & drying." By equating a garden with a munition plant, the propaganda equates not only gardening with manufacturing but also women's work with men's.

Reversing the preceding metaphors of housekeeping as fighting a war, a 1916 advertisement for Campbell's soup begins with the phrase "Your 'first line of defense'—Good food and good digestion!" The advertisement uses the language of battle as the language for maintaining health: "The enemies of robust health have no chance even to *land* on your constitution when its 'coastline' is properly defended" (italics in original). The ad conflates the body and the nation, playing on larger fears to bring attention to the local body, bodies that women can defend.

Women writers participated in the effort to win people over to the Allied cause, often encouraging women to do the work they could do to support the war. In "Poetics of the Frugal Housewife: A Modernist Narrative of the Great War and America," Mark Van Wienen discusses the role of women's poetry as propaganda in influencing the practices of American housewives (1995). Explicitly political poetry written by women poets associated with organizations such as the U.S. Food Administration, the Woman's Peace Party, the Socialist Party, and the Vigilantes[3]—a patriotic writers' organization—was found in a variety of venues, including magazines, newspapers, political tracts, single-author poetry publications, and poetry anthologies (56). Van Wienen shows that housewives were courted by war propagandists as a way to keep Americans submissive to the high food prices and willing to help the war cause (64). Food was ultimately the most important weapon the Allies had; with the soldiers stuck in trenches, each side needed to be able to supply troops with food enough that they could endure a war of attrition. Housewives were therefore "effectively transformed into . . . frontline soldier[s] and placed under military discipline" (65). Van Wienen describes the two attitudes that food propaganda allowed women: a "fecundity responsive only to the state and slavishly obedient to its dictates," an attitude encouraged by propaganda machines such as the Vigilantes (67), or a new sense of empowerment as women's sphere became a significant factor in public life (75).

In general, women's response was to accept the challenges of the latter. Not only were women empowered by their control over the food supply, they took the opportunity to help shape the ideology of war itself. The works this chapter explores are all by and about white, middle-class women; poor women had little choice in practical matters such as food restrictions or buying war bonds since they had no money to choose to spend or not to spend. Yet that women participated in writing novels—propaganda and otherwise—about the war in itself suggests a new role for women. In *The World Wars through the Female Gaze*, Jean Gallagher argues that "[w]hile popular discourse during the world wars, such as recruiting posters, has often tended to reinforce women's position as objects of a male gaze, a culture at war also requires that women be inscribed as seeing-subjects in order to enlist their support for military action" (1998, 11). As "seeing-subjects"—and writing-subjects—women took on a role in society they had previously been denied. In World War I, a war propagandized on a scale not theretofore seen, women became necessary objects of propaganda, but the need that made them objects of propaganda allowed them greater scope in what they could say in response to the war.

The first two novels this chapter discusses, Temple Bailey's *Tin Soldier* (1918) and Ellen Glasgow's *Builders* (1919), were written during the war and emphasize women's role in creating an ideology for war. But the connection between the domestic world and the world of battle is a two-way street; these novels spell out a domestic ideology that relies on, even as it helps to create, an ideology of war. The language and events of war define the home, even as the homemakers prove necessary to men's ability to participate in the war effort. Neither novel, however, is completely comfortable with the implications of the ideology it articulates. The second two novels discussed in this chapter, Glasgow's *Sheltered Life* (1932) and Willa Cather's *One of Ours* (1922), were written after the war and voice a deeper interrogation of the accepted relationship between home and war. Both writers come to question the ideology of home, war, and gender and to recognize the connection between the structure of the home and family and the violence of war.

Temple Bailey's Sentimental Ideology

Women's writing about the war often took the form of sentimental propagandistic work—termed "patriotic potboilers" by Peter Aichinger (1975, 3). Temple Bailey's *Tin Soldier* (1918), for example, portrays a sentimental romance between two idealistic young lovers. As a sentimental novel, it offers readers a set of tools with which to understand the significance of each individual's participation in the war effort; that is, the novel presents a clear-cut sense of right and wrong, good and bad, masculine and feminine as well as describes proper ways of behaving for men and women. The importance of women as "Beautiful Souls" is emphasized, although, significantly, women are not limited to home-front roles. As feminist scholarship has shown us, the First World War provided new options for women, some at home, some at the front. In Bailey's novel, however, women, despite being liberated from staying at home, still remain the ideological repository of beauty and goodness, and they support their men in fighting.

I have identified *The Tin Soldier* as a sentimental novel, a categorization that requires elaboration. June Howard's recent article "What Is Sentimentality?" throws light on the term, exploring its historical constructions and attempting to remove its judgmental associations (1999). In an important critical move, Howard brings together work from a variety of disciplines—sociology, psychology, biology—in order to tease out what sentiment and emotion are, and in doing so she approaches sentimentality without defensiveness or criticism. She points to research that shows emotion and sentiment to be socially created and bodily experienced; Howard argues that sentimentality has evoked discomfort because "the social construction of emotion becomes visible when attitudes about what sensations are appropriate . . . clash . . . . [T]he appearance of the term marks a site where values are contested" (69). Thus to identify *The Tin Soldier* as sentimental reflects not a judgment but a critical interpretation: The novel's emotional excesses not only perform Tompkins's cultural work of influencing popular opinion but also point to a contested terrain, contested not only at the time but also in current critical discourse. Bailey's novel is particularly revealing about the ideological battles in the United States surrounding the First World War *because* it is a sentimental novel, mapping a new system of gender, nationality, and identity.

The Tin Soldier envisions war as both an opportunity for individual growth and a call for self-sacrifice, a means by which the individual can give to the collective. The novel is the story of young lovers, Jean McKenzie and Derry Drake, set during the time just after the United States has entered the war. Jean is a good-hearted but childish, sheltered young woman, while Derry is a wealthy man thought a "slacker" because he has not joined the military. In fact, Derry is bound by a promise to his dead mother to stay home and care for his alcoholic father, General Drake. Other characters include Jean's father, Dr. McKenzie, a well-meaning but fallible doctor; Emily Bridges, a friend of the McKenzie family and surrogate mother to Jean; Drusilla Gray, a modern young woman who takes the initiative and goes to the war; and Hilda Merritt, a self-serving nurse in Dr. McKenzie's employ who displays an unsettling mix of selfishness and practicality.

The novel establishes clearly what is expected of men and of women, especially in relation to the war. Men are to fight, and women, though they do not necessarily have to stay home, are to be guiding angels ("Beautiful Souls") for the men to remember and to fight for. The novel includes a broader range of female characters than it does of male characters, perhaps indicative of the new roles and opportunities the war provided for women but also suggestive of the necessity of women to behave in a certain way and of the danger possible when they do not. The various women characters are still tied to a conventional moral paradigm; they are classified as "good" and "bad," a determination based on the feelings and character they bring out in men. Alma Drew, for example, who refuses to believe that the war is America's business, is consequently rejected by the truly patriotic characters. Hilda Merritt, the self-centered nurse, fascinates Dr. McKenzie but fails to bring out goodness in him; thus she cannot be considered a "good" woman.

The novel shows that the definition of "woman" requires self-sacrifice and a willingness to sacrifice one's men for a noble cause. Jean McKenzie's growth from girlhood into womanhood corresponds directly to her changing attitude toward the war. Nancy Huston points out in "The Matrix of War" that although in general real women do not fight, in legend virgins are able to go to war (1986, 128). It is only when they become actual or possible child bearers that they are excluded from fighting. In *The Tin Soldier* Jean at one time wishes to serve in battle herself: "She had yearned to be a man that she might stand in the forefront of battle" (Bailey 1918, 71). She can argue vehemently with an antiwar speaker, "[r]ising a little in her stirrups, her riding-crop uplifted to emphasize her burning words, her cheeks on fire, her eyes, shining, her hair blowing under her three-cornered hat" (67). As a virgin, Jean resembles the warrior Joan of Arc, with whom she is later identified. But she finds herself tested when the danger of war comes to the men she loves. She easily and gladly endures meatless and wheatless days and gives up her Thanksgiving turkey, but it is only when she begins to love Derry that she starts to grow up: When Derry is scorned for being out of the war, she suffers "not as a child, but as a woman" (135). Jean's attitude toward war is tested by her engagement and marriage. When the time comes for her father to leave, she finds herself feeling what Alma Drew expressed—that Europe should take care of its own problems. She passes into womanhood only when Derry asks whether she loves him enough to let him go; his expectations of her make her able to fulfill those expectations. He needs her to be his strong woman at home, and so she finds the strength to be that woman. At home, she can mean "more to him than she could ever have meant in times of peace, because he could go forth to fight for her, his life at stake, for her" (410). And it is Derry who calls her "Jean-Joan"; unlike the Maid of Orléans, however, Jean fights by being Derry's touchstone in battle, rather than by carrying a weapon herself.

Drusilla Gray too sees the war as a right and glorious enterprise and thus can willingly send her lover to battle. Drusilla literally embodies the "Beautiful Soul" by converting her body into war propaganda: She consistently wears red, white, and blue. At one party "she wore a gown of sheer dull blue, there was a red rose in her hair—her white arms, her white neck, the blue and red, youth and fire, strength and purity" (109). Her body—arms and neck—become something she wears, like the gown and the rose.[4] The whiteness of her skin suggests a disturbing connection between race and patriotism.[5] She also decorates her home in patriotic colors and converts her singing voice into a propaganda tool. This voice she puts to the service of the war, singing "with the crash of battle in the music" (48). By her very body she inspires patriotism, both encouraging men to fight and being the object for which they fight.

More than just a symbol, Drusilla also embodies a new kind of woman, one who takes a more active part in the war. Her passion for the cause allows her to seize opportunities the war has given women. Drusilla goes to France and drives an ambulance from the front lines back to the hospitals. As Jane Marcus points out about upper-class British women, these female ambulance drivers found themselves in an unreal world of dirt, bodily destruction, and decay, and they were marked as oddities, their upper-class background separating them from the accepted status of working-class women and their work as nurses or other volunteers (125). Drusilla is aware of the implications of British women's participation in the fighting, telling her British lover, "Your gentle maidens . . . are driving ambulances or making munitions. When the Tommies come marching home again they will find comrades, not clinging vines" (174). In France Drusilla sees images indicating changes in the world, "men as tender as women, women as brave as men" (360). The war has given both men and women a chance to reverse expectations. And unlike Jean, Drusilla does not fall in love instantly, as a stereotypical character in a sentimental romance, though she has always dreamed of that kind of glorious love. Instead, she comes to love slowly, gradually over time, but when she does her love is no less strong than Derry and Jean's. Through Drusilla, Bailey suggests that there is more than one way to be a woman, but, significantly, Drusilla is still a Beautiful Soul, an icon that sings to the tired soldiers as they return from the front: "[S]he was more to them than a singing woman. Behind her stood a steadfast people—and God was marching on" (456).

The character of the nurse Hilda Merritt shows in more detail the complex expectations women were expected to fulfill. As a nurse, Hilda
should be valued as a caregiver; she goes to the war, like Drusilla, and thus
she should be considered patriotic. Yet the novel consistently places her
in opposition to Jean and Drusilla. Jean knits socks for soldiers; Hilda's
hands "lay idle in her lap" (20). Hilda does, however, have a common-
sense attitude that is appealing, especially to Jean's father, Dr. McKenzie.
She is a pragmatist and an opportunist, taking advantage of the sick, alcoholic General Drake to get him to marry her; although she seems to
embody the ideals of the self-made American, those characteristics are
shown to be unattractive in a woman, especially during war. Hilda's practicality, however, has a sense of justice to it; as she herself says, "If you
stood under a tree and a great ripe peach hung just out of your reach,
could you be blamed for shaking the tree? Well, I shook the tree" (274).
Ultimately, however, Bailey brings home the point that because Hilda's
soul is "distorted" (270) she cannot ever be redemptive. Although she is
an excellent nurse, the doctor rejects Hilda as his head nurse in France
because he believes that her cold, selfish nature could not heal the
wounds the soldiers have suffered: "[W]e have to care here for more than
men's bodies, we care for their minds and souls. . . . I fancy that you see
in every man his particular devil, and like to lure it out for him to look
at—" (374). Idealism, especially in women, triumphs over practicality.

The men rely on women such as Jean and Drusilla for strength and for
inspiration to go to war. Bailey suggests that women can be good or bad,
as defined by their effect on men; men, on the other hand, seem to be uni-
formly good with weaknesses that the wrong woman could bring out and
the right woman could help change. When Alma Drew defends Derry for
not fighting, he reacts with disgust at her selfishness: "If all women
defended men who wouldn't fight, what kind of world would it be?
Women who were worth anything girded their men for battle" (76–77).
Derry later writes Jean that it is what the women think of their men that
"sways us level" (345). For Dr. McKenzie, keeping himself "level" is a
challenge; he claims that if his wife had lived he would not be such a
"weather cock," swaying according to the women around him. Because his
wife is dead, he is susceptible to morally weak women; he relies on his
daughter to "hold [him] to [his] best," yet he finds himself fascinated by
and attracted to Hilda. When he finally brings himself to ask the kind and
loyal Emily Bridges to marry him, he is too late; she has already become
engaged to another man. At the end of the novel Drusilla expresses her
hope that the war will teach the doctor that "women aren't playthings"
(455); as the war remakes gender roles, Drusilla suggests, men must come
to understand that women are more than guideposts for men.

In *The Tin Soldier*, the domestic world is linked directly with the world of battle. Characters rarely discuss or think of the violence of the war; the fear of death is not so great as the horror of the physical discomforts the men at the front endure: hunger, wet, cold, and mud. These problems are the realm of women, and it is the women's concern at home as to how to solve them. Jean knits sweaters and socks, and her father praises her work with the comment, "Did you ever stop to think what it means to a man over there when a woman says 'I'm going to knit socks'?" (19). Mrs. Connolly, a mother with two sons at the front, worries more over her boys' feet than the possibility of their deaths: "I don't mind the fighting as much as I do the chance of their taking cold. And I'm afraid they won't have the sense to change their socks when they are wet" (253). Such worrying gives women something over which they can exert power; for these women war is pictured as housekeeping out of control. Even though this view may seem naïve, it shows women's implication in war as counterparts to soldiers. Both men and women have jobs to do in order to win the fight.

Although the world of war is envisioned by characters in many texts as disrupted domestic space, the foundations of domesticity are directly linked to the experience of war. Family relationships, in Bailey's novel, are firmly tied to military history. General Drake, himself a veteran of two wars, accuses his son of being a slacker, saying that he does not want Derry "dragged" to defend his country (211). Instead he wishes his son to go willingly to war and to fight as he himself no longer can. Military service is a legacy to the son, and for the son a responsibility to the past. In his home Derry sees portraits of his family: "There were other men in uniform— ancestors" (57). By participating in the war Derry participates for his father as well for the long line of ancestors. Ironically, General Drake's alcoholism began during the Civil War, when no medicine was available and troops were given whiskey to dull pain; war has worked itself into the very flesh of the family.

Derry, however, has conflicted responsibilities to the past. His allegiance to his father demands that he fight, but his loyalty to his mother requires that he take care of his father. Before she died, his mother made him promise he would never leave his father because of the General's alcoholism and his tendency to wander off when drunk. When Dr. McKenzie "question[s] whether any promise should stand between a man and his country's need of him" (87), he does not understand the full extent of the problem. Derry envisions his patriotic service as closely related to his familial obligations. To break his promise to his mother would be as bad as avoiding the war. Furthermore, he would have difficulty fighting with a broken promise behind him. At training camp Derry meets a man who remembers doing the washing with his mother, whose "eyes were bright and her cheeks were red"; this is "a memory for a man on the battlefield" (347). Should Derry go to war with a broken promise, images of his mother would haunt rather than sustain him. Luckily Jean steps into the gap, caring for Derry's father so that Derry can go to war. Through marriage Derry fulfills both military and domestic obligations, restoring a balance between those obligations that his promise to his mother had unintentionally disturbed.

In her essay about American women's writings about the First World War, Dorothy Goldman shows that women writers tend to support women's traditional role during wartime, "but this conventional picture in fact embodies radical new perceptions in its suggestion that women's sacrifices are identical to those of their menfolk" (1993a, 189). She argues that in the First World War, women and men shared the war experience as they had not in previous wars, both in ideological and literal commitment. In *The Tin Soldier*, depictions of domestic life include the hardships the war caused. Margaret Morgan, Derry's cousin, runs a strict household in order to help the soldiers abroad, teaching her children to know and understand self-sacrifice. Emily Bridges turns her Toy Shop into a Red Cross station, saying, "I am taking no more chances for future living, than the men who give up everything to fight" (Bailey 1918, 377). Even Derry, trapped at home before he is released from his promise to his mother, gives up eating peaches, reflecting on all the food the men at the front do not get: "no peaches, no squabs, no mushrooms, no avocados—for them bully beef and soup cubes, a handful of dates, or by good luck a bit of chocolate" (57). In *The Tin Soldier*, the war effort is seen as a combined effort at home and at the front.

In the new sharing of experience in the First World War, the notion of sacrifice takes on divergent, gendered meanings. Derry's cousin Margaret, who knows why Derry cannot go to war, complains to her husband that Derry should have to be "sacrificed" by a promise to his mother to remain at home; Margaret believes Derry should be given a chance to fill his role in the war. In this case, "sacrifice" means a man's being kept from filling his desire and duty to enter the war. Ironically Margaret's own husband is "sacrificed"—in the more traditional sense of killed—to the war cause. The novel suggests that for men to be kept from the war is a personal loss; they should instead be given the chance to die for their country and their beliefs. Women, on the other hand, make sacrifices at home when they give up various foods but also, more important, when they give up their men. Derry objects to "sacrificing" Jean to the service of his father and the loneliness of his big house (321), but Jean points out that the war demands sacrifices of everyone. When Derry is "sacrificed" to the home (before he is released from his promise), such a sacrifice seems unfair;

when Jean is "sacrificed" to the dreary Drake home with the ill General, the act is burdensome but not unreasonable. Significantly, Jean's sacrifice to the home allows the possibility that Derry might sacrifice himself in battle. The novel suggests that women's war work is to sacrifice themselves at home. Although to modern readers it may seem that men's and women's sacrifices in the novel are unequal—since, after all, it is the men who risk death—in fact *The Tin Soldier* creates and relies on the sense that these sacrifices are ideologically equivalent.

The novel equates the war work of men and women by breaking down the public/private dichotomy on which the ideology of war and home rest. That is, things that had previously been private become significant elements of public life. Derry and Jean's love for each other is no longer an isolated event: "[T]hey were caught in the tide of that mighty wave which was sweeping the world!" (123) Only after they have stated their love do they become part of the "mighty wave," a communal feeling of sacrifice and ideological commitment. The private and the domestic have become linked to world events, a public exposure that can help negate the horror of the events of war. At the end of the novel Drusilla points out that "[l]ove—in these times, Derry—isn't building a nest. . . . It goes as far as the future of mankind. What the future of the world will be depends not so much on how much you love Jean or how much she loves you, or on how much I loved and was loved, but on how much that love will mean to the world" (452). During war and cultural upheaval, love cannot be kept in a private realm. It embodies the ideals for which a country fights.

The Tin Soldier shows a faith in the importance of idealism—of love and dreams. Although the novel relies on gender stereotypes, such reliance suggests that these stereotypes can make the world a better place; ultimately Dr. McKenzie realizes that the difference between how Jean and Hilda make him feel is important: "It is something to be a hero to one's daughter. Perhaps some day I shall be a little better for her thinking so" (97). And as a whole the novel suggests that idealism can make a difference in world events—a self-referential exercise, since the novel helps create that idealism.

The problematic underside of such idealism is the monstrosity by which the enemy must be characterized. As Stanley Cooperman argues about World War I literature, ideologically the Germans had to be transformed into "the Teutonic Beast" (1967, 23). *The Tin Soldier* reflects the reluctance to call the enemy "Germans," preferring the terms "Huns" and "the Wolf." In fact, the toys Emily Bridges sells are made in Germany, and she later marries a German, who professes outrage at his homeland's barbarism. The novel distinguishes between Germans as people and the inhuman body that has supposedly created the war.

Although the novel, using the tropes of sentimental fiction, seems to rely on simple ideas and equally simple categories of men and women, of good and bad, the text in fact faces complex issues, shows them in their complexity, and leaves them unresolved. The posthumous letter from Derry's mother to her son lays out the importance and inevitability of contradictions:

> Life isn't white and black, it isn't sheep and goats—it isn't just good people and bad people with a great wall between. Life is gray and amethyst, it is a touch of dinginess on the fleece of the whole flock, and the men and women whom you meet will be those whose great faults are balanced by great virtues and whose little meannesses are contradicted by unexpected generosities. (Bailey 1918, 82)

This recognition of complexity and the impossibility of easy categories undermines the ideology that the novel sets up. For example, even though the text emphasizes the importance of women's putting on brave faces and sending their men forth to glory, Jean's fears for both her father and her lover bring up a very real point. War is portrayed as glorious, yet Jean sees the vengefulness it brings out in her father. She fears what the war will do to men:

> Would Daddy and Derry, when they went over, do that? Torture and mutilate? Would they, would they? And would they come back after that and expect her to love them and live with them?
>
> Well, she wouldn't. She would *not*. She would be afraid of them—of both of them. (184)

With this inquiry, the issue is dropped; the problem of possible changes in returning men is never again addressed, for the novel ends with Derry, Drusilla, and Dr. McKenzie in France. But Jean's fears open a wider question: If men change from glorious soldiers to mutilators and torturers, what does that transformation mean for the women who are defined largely by their relationship to their glorious soldiers? What Jean sees but cannot face is her own complicity in murder and death. As part of the domestic ideology intertwined with the ideology of war, women are as implicated in violence as men, a contradiction inherent in the categorization of women as "Beautiful Souls."

These unresolved questions in *The Tin Soldier* characterize the ideology underlying the First World War. How can women be both "nonwarlike" and directly implicated in the fighting? How can women be militarized and remain outside violence? A close look at this text shatters the illusion that women are the repositories of a nonviolent culture. Even as Bailey attempts to inscribe gender roles and to motivate her readers for war, the gendered ideology of war and home slips away—to be questioned more closely in works by other writers.

Ideology and Sacrifice in Glasgow's *Builders*

Ellen Glasgow's 1919 novel *The Builders* addresses questions similar to those of *The Tin Soldier*, particularly those of women's role in the home and the relationship between private life and the public realm. Glasgow started *The Builders* in 1917, during the early stages of her troubled relationship with Henry Anderson, and, according to critics such as Stanly Godbold, Linda Wagner, and Susan Goodman, the political beliefs of *The Builders'* main character David Blackburn show the strong influence of Anderson's own attitudes. Pamela R. Matthews comments that the influence on the novel of another of Glasgow's friends, her longtime companion Anne Virginia Bennett, should not be overlooked (1994). Matthews points out that Caroline Meade, the nurse in *The Builders*, is modeled after Bennett, including the parallel desires between friend and character to go to the war (89). Written during the war itself and while Glasgow was suffering personal losses—the recent deaths of both her favorite sister and her father and the departure of both Anderson and Bennett for the war—the novel does not question the ideology underlying the war as deeply as would Glasgow's later novel, *The Sheltered Life* (1932).

The Builders is the story of Caroline Meade, a young woman who suffered heartbreak years before and has since become a nurse. At the start of the novel, the United States has not yet entered the war in Europe, and Caroline accepts a position as nurse to David and Angelica Blackburn's daughter Letty. Local gossip holds that David mistreats his wife and that Angelica bears his cruelty with meekness and silence. Once in the Blackburn house, however, Caroline gradually comes to realize that Angelica's mild ways and apparent self-sacrifice conceal a scheming, grasping nature and that David's "abusive" behavior is mere rumor, started by Angelica herself. Caroline eventually becomes sympathetic toward David Blackburn and his political goals.

The Builders establishes the role of woman as selfless domestic center but then quickly undercuts this idea. Caroline first learns of Angelica through others, hearing of her as a beautiful, self-sacrificing angel, and before Caroline even meets her employer she finds that Angelica has captured both her imagination and her loyalty. Angelica is positioned initially as the "Beautiful Soul" for whom war is fought; her name indicates that she should be associated with saintly qualities. As Matthews points out, "[t]he almost mythic force of traditional womanhood represented by Angelica is reinforced by the fact that Caroline is in love with the *idea* of Angelica before she even meets her" (1994, 90). Although Caroline only slowly discovers Angelica's true nature, their first meeting hints at Angelica's lack of moral character: "The woman and the room harmonized so perfectly that one might almost have mistaken Angelica for a piece of hand-painted furniture" (Glasgow 1919, 38). Angelica is beautiful but useless, as Caroline notes when, at Letty's sickbed, she tells Angelica, "There really is nothing you can do here" (149). Angelica continues to fill Caroline's dreams of her as the beautiful woman of the house, however, despite increasing evidence to the contrary, and even after experiencing Angelica's selfishness and insensitivity, Caroline still feels a strong bond to the other woman.

Caroline herself is not the perfect woman of the house. She does not let men do her fighting for her; her father died while she was young, and her first lover left her for another woman. Her life has taught her not to rely on men but rather to think of herself independent of relations to men. Her thoughts and the language surrounding her often refer to her life as a battle: "She looked as if she would fight to the death, would wear herself to a shadow, for any one she loved, or for any cause in which she believed" (162). She refuses to allow herself to be marked by the stereotype that women such as Angelica live by. When Angelica's brother Roane Fitzhugh, a drinker and womanizer, begs Caroline to "make me the kind of man you like," Caroline responds scornfully, "I don't doubt that there are a number of good women who would undertake your regeneration, but I like my work better" (200). When he persists in his attentions, Caroline finds herself pushed out of a "civilized," feminine role:

> As she fought wildly to escape, she was possessed not by terror, but by a blind and primitive fury. Civilization had dropped away from her, and she might have been the first woman struggling against attack in the depths of some tropic jungle. "I'd like to kill you," she thought. . . . "I wonder why some woman hasn't killed him before this?" (203)

Roane has lived this long because women are not trained to kill, merely to occupy a role and manipulate men rather than to take direct action.

Caroline's sense of herself as a woman not bound to roles as angel or demon, like Angelica, allows her to participate in the war in a new way. Whereas Angelica succumbs to a social order that expects her to act as, if not be, a Beautiful Soul, Caroline seems to see beyond such limitations. Like Jean and Drusilla in *The Tin Soldier*, Caroline feels that women can participate in and experience the war on similar if not equal terms with men. She believes herself to have inherited her strength equally from her father and her mother, her mother having "fought every minute" (16) to maintain a home under economic hardship. Like Jean McKenzie, Caroline knits sweaters and socks for the men at the front, and like Drusilla she eventually heads to France. Similarly, David Blackburn's sister Mary decides to go to France when she discovers her fiancé has no strength of character; she does not want a man who can be taken away by another woman (261). *The Builders* suggests the coming into being of a new kind of woman, one who looks for substance and is willing to fight for it herself. In doing so, however, Glasgow reinscribes the role of "Beautiful Soul," for, unlike Angelica, Caroline comes to embody the values for which men fight: selflessness, moral rectitude, and personal responsibility.

Domesticity in *The Builders* is a world of deceit and fragility, reflecting the problem of surface in identifying the "good" and "bad" women and the social and political changes that alter such definitions. Angelica's manipulation of David is described in terms of battle, and Caroline as the nurse has only a minor role in the household. Caroline's own home, despite being full of love and goodwill, is perpetually vulnerable to money worries and provides only a small degree of security. The letter informing Caroline that her first lover had left with another woman invaded Caroline's world in the home; she looks around the house, thinking, "It looks so happy, so sheltered . . . and yet unhappiness came up the road, from a great distance, and found me there—" (27). The home is subject to invasion, and Caroline rarely finds herself satisfied for long in her mother's house. She feels the urge to work both to earn money and to prevent herself from dwelling on her losses. Eventually the war leaves Caroline homeless; she cannot stay with the Blackburns, she cannot stay with her mother, and she ends up living at a boarding house while working in the hospital. The breakdown between the public and the private opens up greater opportunities for women, but that freedom comes at the price of extremely low security.

The question of duty becomes complicated for Caroline, who, as a woman, has loyalties to both home and nation. David Blackburn is not conflicted about what his responsibilities are; he knows when he goes to war that he can leave his daughter in capable hands. Caroline, in contrast, wants to go to the war but also to stay with Letty, and she comments that it is "hard sometimes to recognize one's real duty" (289). Caroline acknowledges that "the duty that never stays at home is seldom to be trusted" (ibid.). It is too easy, she finds, to do the "right" thing as a way to hide from responsibilities at home. Roane Fitzhugh, for example, seems to have found his calling in soldiering; Caroline hears that he has done brave deeds (even rescuing a Red Cross dog) and given up drinking, but this bravery cannot erase Roane's earlier caddish behavior. Proper behavior at home is important, even for men.

Like *The Tin Soldier*, *The Builders* emphasizes the notion that one can serve one's country even if one cannot literally fight; the novel shows poor people such as Mrs. Macy giving up her sleep to knit for the soldiers and Caroline's fellow boarders becoming less self-centered at the mere mention of the men at the front. Of Caroline's sisters' plans, Caroline likes her sister Maud's intention to grow and can vegetables the best, for even though her other sisters intend to go to France to serve, Caroline recognizes that the home front must be tended as well. In fact, Caroline believes that the United States is not really "in it" (342) until the war has begun to affect everyday life, when people's lives are touched by food and fuel shortages and by commitment to volunteer work. For Glasgow, the domestic world is the world in which the war becomes real.

Ultimately, David and Caroline sacrifice their chance at happiness with each other for an ideal of war, an ideal that relies on beliefs in the personal and the everyday. David's political beliefs are founded on the idea that the nation is a collection of individuals, and thus the nation can be only as strong as the decency of its citizens. The development of citizens should be the primary goal of the nation; indeed, Angelica serves as a striking example of the selfishness and deceit that arise when the home does not produce honorable citizens. Both Mammy Riah and Angelica's cousin Matty Timberlake claim that Angelica was spoiled as a girl; Matty points out, "the way you're raised seems to become a habit with you" (211). David expands this idea to its implications for the nation, saying "[t]he future of our democracy rests not in the Halls of Congress, but in the cradle; and to build for permanency, we must build, not on theory, but on personal rectitude" (354). Although David's hopes for a public life, putting his ideas into effect on a broad scale, are destroyed by Angelica's selfish maneuverings, he cannot refuse to allow her to return after she has left him but fallen ill. The sacrifices the soldiers are making in France require him, he believes, to sacrifice his personal desires to a larger morality.

Whether David's ideals can withstand the reality of daily life is a question the novel leaves unanswered. As Julius R. Raper points out, "Caroline fails to test these abstractions against Blackburn's reality" (1980, 40); Raper refers to Caroline's inability to separate David as symbol—"of the future, of the South becoming, of southern individualism" (ibid.)—from the daily implications of David's words and actions. Although David is a practical man who believes in the power of personal rectitude, he is also flawed by his inability to spot the undercurrents in his own home. He fails to see Angelica's manipulation of his sister's fiancé; Matty and Caroline must point it out to him. As a man, he is not trained in the powers of perception in individual relationships that make the home either a malignant or a beneficent influence. David is too idealistic to carry out his own ideals. By allowing Angelica to return to her child, he fulfills a social obligation but does no true service either to his daughter or his society. Local gossip will continue to believe in Angelica's goodness, destroying his reputation and subsequently his effectiveness as a public servant. Whereas *The Tin Soldier* suggests that idealism, despite its limitations and contradictions, is a powerful force, *The Builders* implies that idealism that professes to rely on personal responsibility blinds itself to evil. By living according to this code of "personality is everything" (Glasgow 1919, 376), David sacrifices personal happiness for not only himself but also for Caroline. A sense of patriotism and "personal rectitude" that admits no individual happiness leaves much to be desired; despite Caroline's defiance in the face of heartbreak, she longs for love, and her willingness to live the rest of her life with only the memory of her one hour talking with David seems to be an image of a starved dog happy for its single table scrap.

Lacking the possibility of a domestic life, Caroline tries to join David on a different level: "I, too, can build my home on ideas" (334). Like David, however, she risks sacrificing herself to her ideals rather than fulfilling them. If the character of a nation is founded on the personal rectitude of its citizens, then the nation's emotional energy must also come from the citizens; if Caroline and David lack the daily joys of love, by implication the nation will suffer too—a contrast to *The Tin Soldier*, which anticipates a world built on individual love and happiness. In *The Builders*, the failure of domestic ideology to provide a workable model for living suggests a larger threat to national life. Glasgow suggests that the need to restructure domestic values is as important as the need to rebuild the world through war—more important, in fact, since public ideology is based on private life.

The Failure of the Southern Home in *The Sheltered Life*

The question of personal ethics in relationship to the involvement of the United States in World War I is an issue Glasgow returned to later, in her 1932 novel *The Sheltered Life*. The story of the protected upbringing of Jenny Blair Archbald, *The Sheltered Life* explores the connection of the personal to the public. The novel follows the rhythms of the Archbald and Birdsong households, describing daily activities and conversation. Characters act as if the home were a sphere isolated from the changing currents around it, such as women's suffrage and socialism, but ultimately the novel shows that the separation of these worlds is false. Like *The*

Builders, this novel connects personal responsibility to national responsibility for world events.

The Sheltered Life describes the civilization of the South as dependent on the idealization of women, the glorification of their beauty, and their protection from the outside world—a manifestation of Elshtain's idea of women as both collective and individual "Beautiful Souls." Eva Birdsong, a celebrated beauty, allows men to project their ideals onto her and then tries to live up to those ideals, in the process refusing to see her husband's infidelities and killing her inner self. Eva embodies the values that the South fought for in the Civil War, but, significantly, these values, like the war, are lost—if they ever existed; as General Archbald reflects, "life would never again melt and mingle into the radiance that was Eva Birdsong" (Glasgow 1966, 278). Despite this feeling, the Archbalds try to shape Jenny Blair in Eva's image. The General notes that though Jenny Blair is not a great beauty, "she measured up . . . to the less elevated standards of our democracy" (135). The appearance of women is directly politicized: An aristocracy requires beautiful women to represent the superiority of the upper class, whereas a democracy, the General implies, is naturally too unrefined to maintain the superior standards.

Nevertheless, the Archbalds instill in Jenny Blair the illusion that she lives in a protected world. As the novel opens, Jenny Blair is reading *Little Women,* a novel about women's role during wartime, because her grandfather is paying her a penny for each page she reads. This incident reflects the broader way that Jenny Blair is indoctrinated into the South's code of genteel behavior—men's views shape the ideals to which women aspire. The code of gentility often involves using words to make a difficult situation fit into the aristocratic, old-South view of life; for example, Mrs. Archbald tells her daughter: "Aunt Isabella broke her engagement because she was not sure of the state of her feelings. Remember those words—the state of her feelings. If Bena Peyton ever says anything about it, that is what you are to tell her" (68). Jenny Blair comes to believe these lies and, more important, to believe in a world where situations can be changed by what one says about them. Thus she defends herself against implication in George's death with the words "I didn't mean anything in the world!" (292).

Although most of the novel takes place within the sheltered and sheltering home, traces of political and social movements reveal themselves as a significant backdrop to the action. The young doctor John Welch is consistently associated with the socialist and suffrage movements (199), and the men discuss political topics such as foreign affairs and suffrage over the supper table (235). Less obviously, the "odor of decay" (a smell from a chemical plant) sometimes creeps into the homes of the upper class, and when Jenny Blair wanders down the street she sees "warlike but ungallant boys" fighting each other (37). These boys indicate a change from the romanticized, chivalric old South, but they also suggest a grimy reality that has always been present. Later Jenny Blair takes another walk, this time coming across "unsheltered women" (232). Poverty and industrialization are always within sight of the Archbalds' and Birdsongs' privileged homes. Issues of race, too, are never far from the surface, as George Birdsong's African American mistress Memoria enters the houses freely yet almost unseen. In "Memory and Memoria in *The Sheltered Life*," Susan Goodman argues that "first, [Glasgow] commemorates the history [of slavery and war] that Memoria embodies; and second, she reveals the impossibility of separating Memoria's history from that of Jenny Blair and the other women of Queenborough" (1995, 245). Politics—spoken and unspoken—shape the home; the home is defined by what it must be sheltered from.

Even the adolescent Jenny Blair perceives the increasing tension between the restricted Southern genteel life and the social changes about her. She wants to go to New York, she wants to go to the war (Glasgow 1966, 272), she wants to be a suffragette (216), and she wants women to take up smoking in public (157). She ends up doing none of these things. She does, however, recognize the false dichotomy between private and public; when her grandfather objects to her going to New York because of "how many temptations there are in the world to-day," Jenny Blair responds, "But don't they get into the home too?" (133) Consciously or not, Jenny Blair acknowledges the increasingly untenable distinction between the home and the public world.

The social changes of the early twentieth century and the First World War force the Archbalds and the South to reconsider the idea of "civilization." The Old South and its code of gentility literally decay and disintegrate in the physical illness and mental breakdown of Eva Birdsong. As John Welch sees, Eva and George's marriage cannot be separated from George's life with other women. The public and private are integrally related; the home is the breeding ground for the blindness and oppression that cause a decayed civilization. Eva Birdsong's flights out of her house signify the connection between home and social decay: She says to Jenny Blair, "when that terror seizes me, I am obliged to rush out of doors, to get away from myself—or the part of myself that I leave in the house" (284). The breakdown of civilization can be seen as well in the literal deterioration of the Birdsongs' housekeeping. Eva reveals to the General that she has been maintaining her household by selling off china and crystal without telling her husband (148); the domestic world is feeding on its own flesh. Ultimately Eva implodes psychologically and murders her husband. As Raper argues, "Glasgow parallels Eva's fall from idealism into terror and violence with events of 1914 in the world at large. If we are to regard Eva's crime of passion in shooting George as the effect of fear brought on by disillusioned idealism, are we not meant to draw similar but broader inferences" about the conflict between nations; that is, "[w]hen reality finally breaks through the inner walls of idealism, violence bursts forth" (1980, 145).

In *The Sheltered Life*, it is not only Southern civilization "breaking down" with the events leading up to the war. As John Welch says, "our civilization is as good as the rest, perhaps better than most, because it's less noisy, but the whole thing is a hollow crust everywhere" (Glasgow 1966, 219). General Archbald views the war as a "swerv[ing] aside" of "the process men called civilization" (275). The decay of the South is linked to broader fears about Western civilization as a whole: Civilization is represented both as something superficial and as a historical movement, an evolution of culture to a higher state. These notions of civilization reveal a sense of falseness— a sense that civilization is merely an illusion. Jenny Blair's lack of responsibility toward those around her exemplifies the fears John and the General have about civilization: She has no preparation for the controlling of desire that makes a society "civilized." In her relationship with George Birdsong she feels a mindless wanting: "Millions of years before she was born, it must have lain somewhere, that hunger, waiting, wanting, as dumb as the earth or the rocks" (257). This sexual desire, Glasgow suggests, is linked to the human urge to go to war. In John Welch's and General Archbald's sense of civilization as merely superficial, the instinct to fight and the instinct for sex are the forces that both underlie civilization and threaten to overthrow it.

Thus, *The Sheltered Life* suggests a fundamental problem with the idea of civilization and the false security in which people believe in it. Home creates civilization and war destroys it, but the hypocrisy that brings war comes from the home. The home, Glasgow suggests, is the key to preventing war. Civilization must be re-created to include and acknowledge truth about human existence and desire, or, less idealistically, people must come to understand the fragility of civilization and their own responsibilities to the lies on which it is based.

When the Housekeeper Is a Man: Cather's *One of Ours*

Willa Cather's 1922 novel *One of Ours* seems always to have been surrounded by controversy. Cather claimed she did not set out to write a war novel, and the critical reception the novel received seems to indicate she should not have bothered. Ernest Hemingway was one of its harshest critics, claiming that Cather's lack of battle experience excluded her from ever being able to write about war. Yet the novel won a Pulitzer Prize, and current critical discussion still finds the book problematic. An important issue, for example, is the amount of distance to be read into the space between Cather and Claude Wheeler. Cooperman, categorizing *One of Ours* as a "recruiting poster" (1967, 29) and an "idealization of the Crusade" (321), fails to note the irony with which Cather portrays Claude. Although Cather identified strongly with Claude when writing the novel, particularly because of her fondness for the cousin on whom she based Claude, critics such as Sharon O'Brien and D. A. Boxwell argue that the identification between author and subject is neither complete nor consistent. Boxwell emphasizes that *One of Ours*, as a modern novel, must be read with an eye to its irony (1994).

My interest here is the ways in which the ideology of home and the ideology of war come together in this novel. The novel's distance and ironic attitude toward the beliefs of the characters force a continual reevaluation of those beliefs. Like *The Sheltered Life*, *One of Ours* was written and published after the First World War; it was never intended to be a propaganda piece for war. It is a novel about the home and the home's relationship to the larger world—in particular a world preparing for and engaged in war. What O'Brien calls Cather's "combat envy" made her want to understand what made a man go to war and how war changed him (1989); the novel shows the ideological forces affecting one American soldier in the time leading up to and during World War I.

One of Ours is filled with descriptions of houses, food, cleaning, and family life.[6] The family routine seems to revolve around food, and the Wheeler house is carefully described, especially the kitchen and the living room (Cather 1922, 42). In contrast is the house where Claude boards when he goes to school; Annabelle chants lessons while cleaning "until Claude feared he would always associate [Horace] with the heaviness of hurriedly prepared luncheons" (29). One of the first homes to make a positive impression on Claude is the Erlichs', where people come and go, lively discussions occur, and people are not afraid to argue:

> On a table in the middle of the room were pipes and boxes of tobacco, cigars in a glass jar, and a big Chinese bowl full of cigarettes. This provisionment seemed the more remarkable to Claude because at home he had to smoke in the cow shed. The number of books astonished him almost as much; the wainscoting all around the room was built up in open bookcases, stuffed with volumes fat and thin, and they all looked interesting, and hard-used. (35)

The novel also describes the homes of the French people Claude boards with or visits; Claude is billeted with a welcoming French family who remind him of Mahailey and the farm (282). The novel relies on place, particularly homes, to express Claude's need for belonging and his sense of alienation.

In Claude's experience, love is expressed in terms of housekeeping; unlike his brothers and father, Claude recognizes and values the emotion that motivates household labor and that can be represented by an ordinary object. Mrs. Wheeler, powerless to prevent her husband's embarrassing Claude by making him drive the old wagon and mules to town with the hired hands, offers to "do up" his linen coat (6); when Claude rejects this overture he sees that his mother is hurt, and to make up for his rudeness he lets his mother put out a clean shirt for him. This exchange is the only way the two can comfort each other—by offering and accepting household labor. In addition, Claude fixes tools for the housekeeper, Mahailey: "[W]hen she broke a handle off her rolling pin, he put on another, and he fitted a haft to her favorite butcher-knife after everyone else said it must be thrown away. These objects, after they had been mended, acquired a new value in her eyes, and she liked to work with them" (21). Claude understands the value of household items and that they come to acquire that value through the work of someone one loves. Mahailey expresses her love for Claude by hiding the pickled peaches, which she made just for him, from his brother Ralph. When Mr. Wheeler, who does not easily express affection and even delights in tormenting Claude, does show feeling for his son, he does so by giving him money to buy his new wife something she might want.

When the war begins in Europe, it gradually comes to take a central place in the household ritual. Claude and his mother read the war news in the evening after the day's work is done. The war affects more homes than just the Wheelers'; the night the Grand Duke is murdered, "on many prairie homesteads, the women, American and foreign-born, were hunting for a map" (133). The war opens up the world of the household as they learn geography (even Claude, who had been to the university, "seemed to have some vague idea that [Luxembourg] was a palace" [133]). Further, the war threatens a way of life and housekeeping itself: "[e]ven to these quiet wheat-growing people, the siege guns before Liège were a menace; not to their safety or their goods, but to their comfortable, established way of thinking" (137). Mrs. Wheeler and Mahailey spend time collecting war pictures and stories. And when the war news is bad, Mrs. Wheeler cleans house, "thankful to be able to put some little thing to rights in such a disordered world" (144). The home's rhythms are altered by the war and simultaneously offer a means for releasing the tension the war causes.

The vision of war in the Nebraska part of the novel suggests that war is mainly a disruption of normal household functionings. As in *The Tin Soldier*, characters view the war as housekeeping gone awry, but the images in *One of Ours* focus particularly on the effects of war for women.[7] For Mahailey, the only way to understand the war is through the images she sees of women without homes. She keeps a poster in the kitchen, and through its image she makes meaning of the war: "There she is, huntin' for somethin' to cook with; no stove nor no dishes nor nothin'—everything all broke up. I reckon she'll be mighty glad to see you comin'" (206). Not only is the woman in the poster perhaps starving, but she lacks the tools with which to do her work. This war is different from the other war Mahailey has seen, the Civil War, in its brutality to women and children: "[M]any a time our house was full of Northern soldiers, an' they never so much as broke a piece of my mudder's chiney" (177). Although this may be a romanticized view of the Civil War, Mahailey believes Claude is fighting for other homes and other housekeepers like herself. Even Leonard Dawson, who at first feels the European war is none of America's business, changes his mind and leaves to fight because of "Belgium, the Lusitania, Edith Cavell" (194).[8] This attack on homes, Americans, and women is too much for American men.

But in *One of Ours* the acts of housekeeping—cooking, cleaning, and sewing—are actually threatened by changes much closer to home. The American economy is shifting from one of self-sufficiency to that of an interdependent capitalism; Claude notes with anger and disgust how orchards are left untended simply because people can drive into town and buy fruit. As Claude thinks:

> The farmer raised and took to market things with an intrinsic value; wheat and corn as good as could be grown anywhere in the world. . . . In return he got manufactured articles of poor quality; showy furniture that went to pieces, carpets and draperies that faded, clothes that made a handsome man look like a clown. (84–85)

The machinery that Ralph thinks of as progress only adds more work to his mother's load because she does not understand how the new machines work. In his resistance to both the new machinery and the new economy, Claude acknowledges a problem, but his rejection of the new fails to address the real issues the new products represent.

As several critics point out, Claude lives in an idealized world, a romanticized world that is nostalgic for an earlier time. He lives on a postsettlement prairie, post–*My Antonia* and *O Pioneers!*, a world that seems to offer no new challenges. Claude considers going to South America in search of opportunities, to prevent the "waste of power" (100) he sees in his own energy and youth. With an intellectual life at the university blocked to him, he throws himself into farming and then marriage in the hopes that a "traditional" life will satisfy his dreams of a fulfilling life. Boxwell argues that Claude is forced to marry by the heterosexual economy that allows no other option (1994, 297). Claude's view of marriage itself is idealized; he believes Enid to be a restorative woman, a "Beautiful Soul" who should devote her energies to "missionary work at home"—that is, to Claude himself: "When he was with her, he thought how she was to be the one who would put him right with the world and make him fit into the life about him. . . . His marriage would be the first natural, dutiful, expected thing he had ever done. It would be the beginning of usefulness and content" (Cather 1922, 122). Despite warnings from Enid's father that marriage is not what Claude believes it to be, Claude enters the institution hoping that it will make Enid into a proper, loving woman and himself into a satisfied, happy man.

Part of the problem in Claude and Enid's marriage is Claude's inability to see the reality behind his views of marriage and the fact of Enid herself. To bring about the womanly change in Enid, Claude spends much energy focusing on the home in which he and Enid will live. Unfortunately, Enid's coolness leaves Claude with the house itself rather than with the love that will build a home: "He lavished upon the little house the solicitude and cherishing care Enid seemed not to need" (145). Patricia Lee Yongue points out that Claude fails as a husband because he attempts to limit Enid's ambitions and goals (1988). Even before their marriage, Claude views Enid's actions always in relation to himself; when Enid insists on driving home through the storm, Claude asks her, "What made you so pig-headed? Did you want to frighten me? Or to show me how well you could drive?" Whereas Claude's question focuses on the connection between her action and himself, Enid's response shows her lack of focus on Claude at all: "Neither. I wanted to get home" (Cather 1922, 114). Enid's assumption of agency is something Claude fails to recognize, and consequently he marries her without understanding that she has a will of her own that does not correspond to his. Enid has her own car, and her mobility gives her much more freedom than Claude's mother has. Boxwell claims quite rightly that Enid is too modern to be "contain[ed]" in the domestic world (1994, 298). Claude's inability to see that a woman can fill more than one role or have a self apart from a relationship to a man is part of the reason for the marriage's failure.

It is important to note that, despite her political activity, Enid does not let the house suffer. She always has supper ready for Claude, even if the food comes from cans, and she willingly does his laundry, telling him "he need not economize in working shirts; it was as easy to iron six as three" (Cather 1922, 172). Wearing white dresses as she cleans, Enid runs her house "easily and systematically" (171). But her housekeeping lacks passion; unlike Mahailey and Claude's mother, Enid does not see the love household labor embodies. It is Claude who puts in the emotional energy required to make a house a home, though he necessarily fails since that effort takes two. When he tells Enid bitterly, "All the time you were campaigning, I played housekeeper here" (182), he is referring not so much to the cooking and cleaning, which Enid in fact does, as he is to the care and devotion he has put into his house and his marriage. Cather suggests that housekeeping is not simply mechanical work but activity done out of love, filled with meaning because of the relationships of the people in the house.

Because Claude does not find meaning or fulfillment in his home life, he joins the army; critics have offered several interpretations of this action. Susan J. Rosowski argues that Claude joins the army in order to "give himself up to something more powerful than himself" (1986, 110); he finds his family in the army and he can be free from gender conventions (112). Blanche H. Gelfant argues similarly that Claude goes to war because he longs for a fulfilling family life (1988), and Yongue claims that Claude in his romantic vision sees a "continuity" (1988, 150) between home and war. Boxwell shows that Claude's desire to fulfill the homosocial relationships he has with men leads him to desire an all-male community (1994). All of these critics point out that Claude can find a role as a housekeeper in the army, free from gender restrictions, and a place in a body united by familial ties.

Claude's relationship to the domestic world prepares him for the ideological context of war. Gelfant notes the large number of references to Claude's desire for "something," a vague undefined term (1988). She interprets the "something" to mean family life, but that explanation can be expanded to mean a sense of inclusion in something larger than himself. Claude desires his life to have meaning, which he believes it can have only by his participating in a family that carries on tradition or in an army that will alter the course of history. This "idea" for which the men go to war is vague, but for Claude "[i]deals were not archaic things, beautiful and impotent; they were the real sources of power among men" (Cather 1922, 339). It turns out that Claude himself, and not the women, is the Beautiful Soul of the novel,[9] a complication that both represents the intertwining of home and war and overthrows the ideological underpinnings of both. Like The Tin Soldier and The Builders, One of Ours shows a conflicted relationship toward ideals and idealism. After Claude's death his mother is glad he cannot see the results of the war, though she recognizes that the soldiers "in order to do what they did had to hope extravagantly, and to believe passionately" (370). Yongue argues that Cather shows "war, and its virtual celebration by our society and by Claude Wheeler" are the problem (1988, 152). Yet we have the sense that without those ideals the United States would not have entered the war, and in One of Ours Cather never questions U.S. participation in World War I.

She thus establishes a contradiction: that we need ideals in order to effect change in the world and that idealism can be a cover for corruption and therefore must be questioned.

Conclusion

The ideological system of gender created by the demands of mobilizing the United States for the First World War added a twist to the interdependency of gender dynamics. Because of the needs both for emotional commitment to the war and for food on a massive scale to support the troops abroad, women became, ideologically, equal participants with men in the war effort. Yet they were still held as objects for which men fought, and consequently they had new opportunities as well as familiar restraints. Their writings, like the works of men, reveal a sense of conflict about the nation's commitment to the war, the gender definitions inscribed by war propaganda, and the role of the home in preparing to send men to war. Bailey, Glasgow, and Cather all saw a new relationship between the public and the private brought about by the changing ideology of gender and war.

The war ideology established to win people's commitment to the cause also receives conflicted treatment from these writers (and will be seen to be highly contentious in writings about frontline experiences). Although the question of what the result of World War I would have been if the United States had not entered it is beyond the scope of this project, to dismiss Jean McKenzie, Derry Drake, David Blackburn, and Claude Wheeler as simply idealistic, with the corresponding implication that they have little understanding of reality, is to dismiss the profound impact such idealists and the creators of idealism have had on world history. Such figures are both the result and the makers of an ideology that permeates American culture. Where would the United States be ideologically if we had refused to enter the war? Historical scholars debate this question, but viewed from a cultural and literary standpoint the question seems moot. Americans were set up, as it were, so that their understanding of themselves at home depended on participation in the war; even though opposition to the war was vocal, for the majority of Americans the war was defined in terms they could not refuse. The American sense of identity, highly gendered, was tied explicitly to commitment to the war. Only after the war could writers such as Glasgow and Cather interrogate the ideological illusions that instigated U.S. participation in the First World War.

Chapter 2
Parents and Soldiers:
Incest and Experience

During World War I, the formulation of the ideology of war, especially in its relation to the ideology of the home, reflected and created relations between parents and soldier sons as well as between men and women. Mothers were expected to be the source of the son's patriotism; former president Theodore Roosevelt wrote in one of his many editorials published in the *Kansas City Star* that "[w]omen who do not raise their boys to be soldiers when the country needs them are unfit to live in this republic" (quoted in Ross 1996, 176). Similarly, in Temple Bailey's *Tin Soldier*, one character states that it is the women of France who have held off the Germans because "they are the mothers of men" (1918, 197). Mothers represent and transmit the world of ideals to their children, and in times of war this role is perceived as uniquely important.

Edna Ferber's 1919 short story, "The Maternal Feminine," for example, tells the story of Sophy Decker, an independent, intrepid maiden aunt who has served as mentor to the children of her self-centered sister Flora. Sophy's nephew is killed in World War I, and his nurse comes to visit the family after the war is over. On entering the room where Sophy, Flora, and the family are waiting, the nurse goes directly to Sophy, assuming from Sophy's face that she is the mother. In this story motherhood is defined by love, respect, and support for the "son" rather than by biology; it takes character to create a soldier. The mother represents the origin of the soldier's participation in and commitment to American society and thus ideologically could be equated with patriotism and duty, though for the same reasons she could also be a point against which the son rebelled (for example, Mrs. Krebs in Hemingway's "Soldier's Home"[1]).

The expectations placed on women and soldiers were strikingly similar. In "The Matrix of War," Nancy Huston explores a variety of myths about and cultural standards for child-bearing women and soldiers (1986). She argues that "the symbolic equivalence between childbirth and war might be said to be one of the rare constants of human culture" even while she maintains that "they have traditionally been perceived as mutually exclusive" (127). In her social and historical study *Women and War,* Jean Bethke Elshtain points out that "the soldier is expected to sacrifice for his country as mothers are expected to sacrifice for their children" (1987, 222). Mothers and soldiers experience the same burdens of duty and guilt as well as face mortal danger in fulfilling their responsibilities. In this way mothers, not, as might be expected, fathers, influence the son's conduct in war—not just as transmitters of cultural values but as actual models for behavior.

Some women actively sought to participate in World War I through their role as mothers of soldiers. At the 1916 Republican National Convention suffragettes carried the slogan "For the Safety of the Nation To the Women Give the Vote/For the Hand that Rocks the Cradle Will Never Rock the Boat!" (ibid., 145); in this way the suffrage movement aligned motherhood with patriotism and implied that the nation would be *more* secure because women would vote *against* change. In 1918 the Connecticut State Council of Defense issued "The Ten Commandments of Womanhood," which were assembled by the president of the Connecticut Congress of Mothers. The commandments include injunctions against wasting time, substance, and bread and against personal vanity and lavish dress as well as encouragements to "hearten thy men and weep not, for a strong woman begetteth a strong man, and the blasts of adversity blow hard and swift across the world." The Ten Commandments of Womanhood suggest that propaganda creates— even more than reflects—women's "proper" response to war. The importance of mothers to their soldier sons is indicated as well by popular images of mothers, including songs titled "You're the Greatest Little Mothers in the World (Mothers of America)" and "A Soldier's Rosary." The cover of "A Soldier's Rosary" depicts a soldier writing a letter by firelight and from the letter balloons out an image of his strong, loving mother.[2]

This cult of patriotic motherhood had its negative side, of course. As Kathleen Kennedy shows in her study *Disloyal Mothers and Scurrilous Citizens,* the social changes brought about by the war facilitated an increase in women's public and political visibility, but at the same time "the meanings attached to that increased participation confined women's access to key components of citizenship, such as patriotism and Americanism, to narrow constructions of maternalism" (1999, 3). World War I espionage laws

> assumed that all men of a particular age were potential soldiers and that all women acted as mothers in their relationships with such men. If utterances critical of the war even had the potential to reach men of that age group, juries would convict under the Espionage and Sedition Acts, even if there was no evidence that those utterances specifically targeted draft-aged men. (xvi)

Thus, Kennedy demonstrates, women who were active in the pre-war progressive movements, including the suffrage movement, could be and were prosecuted for advancing their causes on the grounds that they were traitors to their country, and often the accusations against them were directed at these women's refusal to be "mothers," literally or figuratively.

This study, however, addresses the national ideal of women and motherhood. Domestic stories were one way propaganda organizations helped shape attitudes toward the war. In 1917 Doubleday, Page and Company published a short narrative called *The Whistling Mother*, written by Grace S. Richmond, a member of the pro-war writers' group the Vigilantes. A work openly put forth by this group, *The Whistling Mother* targets mothers, describing the soldier's proper hawkish attitude toward the war and the mother's role in her son's military life. The text narrates the final trip home of a young man who has decided to enlist in the army and his relationships with each family member, particularly his "whistling mother."

The work distinguishes between the "wrong" kind of mother and the "right" kind. Upon hearing of her son's enlistment, the wrong kind of mother "would be sick in bed about it, and she'd cling round his neck and cry on his shoulder, and he'd have to loosen her arms and go off leaving her feeling like that" (6). This mother shows her weakness in her inability to release him on her own, to make the sacrifice willingly. Here is the opposite of what Derry Drake writes Jean in *The Tin Soldier* about "a memory for a man on the battlefield"; the wrong kind of mother leaves her son with feelings of guilt that can threaten his ability to perform as a soldier. In contrast, Jack's mother writes him that he should not worry that his trip home will undermine his resolve: "You needn't fear we shall make it hard for you—not we. We may offer you a good deal of jelly, in our enthusiasm for you, but you could always stand a good deal of jelly, you know, so there's no danger of our making a jellyfish of you" (8). She employs a domestic metaphor for the family's ability to help him buck up, not weaken. The family, she knows, is the source of the soldier's strength.

Jack's mother is the example of the right mother, the mother who understands her country's need for her son and, more important, how her own actions and attitudes can be translated into the strength of a soldier. When Jack arrives home, his mother listens "just exactly as another fellow would" and responds, "Why, if you didn't want to go, Jack, I should feel that I'd been the wrong sort of mother" (14). She is not unaware of the reality of war, but she is prepared to face the dangers just as the soldiers themselves are; when she comes to say her private good-bye to her son, her hands "were clinched tight at her sides, just the way I've often clinched mine before I went into a game on which a good deal depended" (24). In this way the narrative shows that the soldiers are not the only players in the game of war. The nation must be mobilized as a whole for the country to bring itself to fight, and even though mobilization starts with the young men, it also includes the families. Preparing her sons for the event of war is part of the mother's job; as Jack points out, on his departure his mother does not need to pray over him and give him advice because she has been doing that all of his life. Teddy Roosevelt would have approved.

Connections between mothers and sons stem partly from traditional roles in which women, as mentioned earlier, played the part of "Beautiful Souls," the locus of all pure values that the soldiers were to defend. Like the wife or girlfriend, the figure of the mother was a unique point against which the soldier defined himself. A pamphlet titled "Mother's Day 1918," produced by the YMCA and available to soldiers to send home to their mothers,[3] includes several tributes to mothers:

> Far, far away we said good-bye to her, but she would not be left behind: she is with us, always with us. "God could not be everywhere, so he gave us Mother." We had boasted to ourselves that we were men, no longer held by apron-strings; and now we find it true, for the strings are become chains, and we are proud of our shackles. Who would have guessed from knowing us that Mother sits throned in our hearts? But there she is, the one who knows us best, the one who counts upon us most, and by her very expectations makes us men such as we had not dreamed to be.

The soldier needed a representative of home and domestic ideology to support him, and the wife/girlfriend figure had liabilities the mother did not. The girlfriend/fiancée, for example, could break off with her soldier lover in favor of another man (Cicely Saunders in Faulkner's *Soldiers' Pay*; Mabe in Dos Passos's *Three Soldiers*; Ellen in Boyd's *Through the Wheat*). The mother would never break off with her son in this way, and thus she becomes a stand-in for the girlfriend/wife.

The interchangeability of mother/wife/girlfriend during war suggests that war brings out what Freud saw as the inherently incestuous nature of the mother/son relationship. Freud's Oedipal triangle describes a competition between father and son for the mother's attention; Freud argues that the son, in effect following in his father's footsteps, wishes to remove the father and take the mother for himself, all in an attempt to "get free" of the father (1963a, 42). In "A Special Type of Object Choice Made by Men" (1910) Freud describes some of the characteristics of "normal" male love: "[T]he libido has dwelt so long in its attachment to the mother, even after puberty, that the maternal characteristics remain stamped on the love objects chosen later—so long that they all become easily recognizable mother-surrogates" (1963b, 53). One of the primary characteristics of the mother is that she always belongs to the father. The son's "instincts, the loving, the grateful, the sensual, the defiant, the self-assertive and independent" are all geared toward a desire for having intercourse with the mother and producing a son: "the wish to be *the father of himself*" (57). The girlfriend/wife is only ever a stand-in for the mother; thus, the mother acting as the son's "Beautiful Soul" in effect reveals the desires that Freud understood to be fundamental to adult sexuality—significantly, a sexuality that is exclusively heterosexual.

While soldiers are headed off to the all-male world of the military and war, the ideology behind them relies on an assumption of sexuality that denies homosexuality. Even today, the "problem" of gays in the military remains highly contested. The ideology of the First World War relied on an implied heterosexuality, even to the extent that images of incest seem acceptable. For example, *The Whistling Mother* suggests that even though the mother's job is to be part comrade, part coach, the mother also fills the role of lover. The language of the narrative and the exchanges between Jack and his mother are oddly in the style of a romance. Jack gazes at his mother sitting in the firelight, a scene reminiscent of a lovers' meeting (Richmond 1917, 17); to say goodnight she comes into his room in "some kind of a loose, rosy sort of silk thing" (20). Jack's comments about his mother equate her with a girlfriend or lover: "Mother's great to hug, just exactly like a girl" (20); "if you don't think she's a peach in an evening dress you never saw her. Her neck and shoulders . . . " (28). Their final private good-bye scene too is highly physical: "[H]er arms were round my neck in the old way, and she was holding me so tight I could hardly breathe—and I don't believe she could breathe much, either, for I was giving her back every bit of that, with some to spare. . . . She didn't keep me long. Just that one great hug, and something else that goes with it" (24). The coyness of this scene again suggests a romantic relationship. This conflation of mother with lover reflects the need for a girl at home who will never leave him for another man since, after all, she already has. In this incestual way, the mother is a figure of emotional security.

In such war texts, family dynamics shift when the son is called to military duty. The son can bear arms, assuming one of the primary male prerogatives, whereas the father must remain home with the women and children. In *The Whistling Mother,* Jack can fulfill the dictates of manhood in ways his father no longer can: "[Dad] was banking on doing his bit in the Home Defence League, and the Red Cross, and everywhere else he could get his hand in, and I could tell well enough that he was aching to be in active service" (30). Although Jack is not gloating in this passage, he clearly understands that his ability to serve in the military is a privilege that

Figure 3. "Good-Bye Dad." Photograph courtesy of the Archives and Special Collections, University of Nebraska-Lincoln Libraries

neither women nor older men can share. A poster for war bonds shows a soldier and his father shaking hands; the caption reads: "Good Bye, Dad. I'm off to fight for Old Glory. You buy U.S. Gov't Bonds."

The father, in this poster, looks old enough to be the son's grandfather—perhaps a veteran of the Civil War—eliminating from public view the generation of men that never fought a war (too young for the Civil War, too old for World War I). Even though propaganda and novels such as *The Tin Soldier* suggest that men's fighting and women's home-front work are equivalent, *The Whistling Mother* and the war-bonds poster indicate that men's home-front work is a poor substitute for soldiering. War aggravates the Oedipal situation, changing the balance of power toward the mother/son alliance. But, simultaneously, the son cannot ever banish the father, and in fact the mother is left behind with the father when the son leaves. At the same moment that the son seems to gain the mother, he loses her.

Although these war texts suggest that a soldier's heightened reliance on his mother comes from his need for a reliable emotional touchstone, the mother's reasons for playing into the mother/lover role seem less clear. Perhaps she is aware of her son's need for her, yet she seems to have her own reasons for her part in this mother/soldier dynamic. In *The Whistling Mother*, the mother dresses to please her son: "[S]he'd gone back to the clothes that make her look like a jolly girl, and I knew she'd done it so I could remember her that way" (28). In *The Tin Soldier*, we saw a dynamic that created an interdependent sense of identity between a young husband and wife; they were each defined by the other's performance of his or her role. When the soldier is not a husband but a son, the wife/mother draws her sense of identity from the son: "Notions of male heroism being important to the aggressive mother, she would have them exemplified in her husband, her son. Honor comes to her through her son; less directly, through her husband" (Elshtain 1987, 192). A poem by Griffin called "To My Son" in the "Mother's Day 1918" pamphlet epitomizes Elshtain's argument:

> Remember the world will be quick with its blame,
> If shadow or stain ever darken your name;
> "Like Mother, like son" is a saying so true,
> The World will judge largely of Mother by you.
>
> Be yours then the task, if task it shall be,
> To force the proud world to do homage to me;
> Be sure it will say when its verdict you've won,
> "She reaped as she sowed, lo, this is her Son."

Since the mother has educated, even created, her son in her society's moral and cultural values, war is the time when her work is tested.

The idealized and propagandistic images of motherhood, fatherhood, and soldiers were called into question after the war by authors such as Cather and Wharton. Both women saw young men sacrificed for an ideology that became hollow. The purported German atrocities were proved to be fabricated; thus not only was the fighting itself a topic that continued to need discussion, in particular by those male authors who took part, but the ideology that enveloped soldiers and noncombatants alike needed to be addressed. The nature of relationships between soldiers and their families was a dynamic that continued to trouble these authors. Cather and Wharton, though both childless women, may have tackled such a topic because, as members of Western civilization, they felt themselves implicated in the violence of the First World War; writing about the parents' point of view allowed them to interpret and address a larger issue—the ideological assumptions underlying the war.

Evangeline and Claude: Cather's Ideological Incest

Written after the war, Cather's *One Of Ours* is not a propaganda piece like *The Whistling Mother*; rather, the novel looks back on the unique relationship of mother and soldier, speculating on their interdependencies for emotional support and self-definition. Cather also interrogates the ideological underpinnings that isolate the mother as the source of values and patriotism and probes family dynamics that seem to align mother and son so closely. Susan Rosowski shows that Cather read the letters that her cousin, G. P. Cather, who was killed in the war, wrote to his mother; Cather also interviewed soldiers and read their diaries (1986, 95). This research suggests that the resulting novel would be flavored by how soldiers viewed their mothers and how they wished to present themselves. In *One of Ours*, Cather shows the strength the son takes from his mother, entangling them both in his ideological investment.

Throughout the novel Claude is closer to his mother than he is to any other family member, but their relationship is not an easy one. The Wheeler family operates according to seemingly odd principles: The outspoken and rough Mr. Wheeler favors the effeminate and prissy son Bayliss; the meek and religious Mrs. Wheeler aligns herself with Claude, who, though easily embarrassed, is the physically strong son, suited bodily if not intellectually for farming. These pairings are based on similarities of personality—Bayliss, like his father, is a hard-headed businessman and has a tendency for snide remarks. Claude and his mother are both more sensitive and therefore are often targets of Mr. Wheeler's brutal sense of humor. But they have divergent inner lives; Claude is interested in more critical academic pursuits, while Mrs. Wheeler relies on her religious faith. This difference leaves Claude feeling that he cannot always understand or be understood by his mother.

Part of the family dynamic consists of an unexplored tension between Claude's parents. Although Nat Wheeler directs his "humorous" attacks at any family member who seems weak, his relationship with his wife is complicated by sexual overtones. When Evangeline complains that she cannot pick cherries because of her bad back, Nat cuts down a cherry tree as a "practical joke" (Cather 1922, 24). This violent response to her complaint suggests insensitivity but also an attempt to establish dominance. The power play between married adults catches the young Claude in the middle; he has accompanied his mother to pick the cherries and so is also a discoverer of the destroyed tree. By throwing a tantrum, he forces his mother to argue for his father's right to cut down the tree and thus to batter his wife emotionally. Claude learns that his father's power over his mother is far greater than his own; she tells him, "I'd rather have the whole orchard cut down than hear you say such things [about your father]" (25). Through his father's violent act Claude discovers both that his claim on his mother is secondary and accordingly that he cannot protect her from that violence.

This scene foreshadows, perhaps necessitates, Claude's eventual enlistment in the army. By cutting down the cherry tree, Nat Wheeler proves to Claude that violence is a necessary part of manhood and effectively threatens his son with the violence and power of adult masculinity. The tree, which "lay on the ground beside its bleeding stump," is a classic Freudian image of castration. Although Claude fears the power of his father, he also resents and judges him, believing that "God would surely punish a man who could do that" (25). At the same time, however, Claude has high expectations for his father; Claude "unreasonably wanted his father to be the most dignified, as he was certainly the handsomest and most intelligent, man in the community" (24). Nat's mild tendency to sadism, reflected in his desire to "harden" both his wife and his son, infuses a fascination with violence in his quiet son. Claude grows up feeling closer to women, protecting the elderly Mrs. Voight from taunting boys, but at the same time he is drawn toward sanctioned violence, such as sports and war. Unable to feel himself an adult under his father's taunting gaze, Claude joins the army. He loses his mother through his father's violence, so it seems that only violence of his own will win her back and establish his own manhood. In this way Claude can become, as Freud says, "the father of himself."

Although the cherry tree incident makes clear to Claude that his mother belongs to his father in a way that she cannot belong to Claude, Mrs. Wheeler does not find emotional intimacy with her husband. It is a relief for both mother and son when Nat Wheeler leaves for the winter to work on the family's other ranch. During his absence Mrs. Wheeler and Claude settle into peaceful domesticity, like a married couple. Claude seems to become the husband Mrs. Wheeler wishes she had; she tells her son, "It's almost like being a bride, keeping house just for you, Claude" (67). Their only serious difference lies in Mrs. Wheeler's profound Christian belief, a faith that Claude cannot share. After one discussion over this difference, however, Claude and his mother "clung together in the pale, clear square of the west window, as the two natures in one person sometimes meet and cling in a fated hour" (73). Despite their divided opinions on religion, the text indicates that Mrs. Wheeler and Claude are a more intimate couple than either Nat and Evangeline or Claude and his wife Enid. The "two natures in one person" imagery suggests the joining and complementarity, in a heterosexual system, of masculine and feminine, where the masculine represents physicality and reason and the feminine represents spirituality and morality. It also recalls the Christian vision of marriage: "And they twain shall be one flesh: so then they are no more twain, but one flesh" (Mark 10:8).

Claude's life revolves around other mother figures as well: the housekeeper Mahailey, the German Mrs. Voight, and Mrs. Erlich. Mrs. Erlich in particular comes closest to rivaling Mrs. Wheeler in Claude's affections. Although Claude visits the Erlich house on the pretext of his friendship with Julius and his brothers, it is Mrs. Erlich that he most enjoys being with. He escorts her to football games and is her chosen companion to the family's opera party. Mrs. Erlich offers intellectual conversation that Mrs. Wheeler, trapped for years on the farm and limited by her religious beliefs, cannot provide, and Claude feels disloyal to his mother for enjoying the other woman's company so much (Cather 1922, 71). His guilt over this betrayal emphasizes the intimate nature of his relationship to his mother—like a man caught in adultery.

The novel suggests that older women, mothers and mother figures, have the strongest moral and philosophical influence on young men. Mrs. Wheeler's religious values have a profound influence on her son, even if he does not share her faith; critic Blanche H. Gelfant, in fact, blames her for encouraging Claude to go to war (1988, 92). Certainly Mrs. Wheeler takes a strong stand on the issue of the war, indignantly replying to Claude's discussion of the difficulties of transporting an army across a German-submarine-infested ocean:

> I don't pretend to say what we could accomplish, son. But we must stand somewhere, morally. They have told us all along that we could be more helpful to the Allies out of the war than in it, because we could send munitions and supplies. If we agree to withdraw that aid, where are we? Helping Germany, all the time we are pretending to mind our own business! If our only alternative is to be at the bottom of the sea, we had better be there! (Cather 1922, 188)

Janis Stout points out that Mrs. Wheeler is the epitome of the propaganda-infused mother, and "in that . . . she is more a victim caught up in a process driven by profit motives (such as her husband's) than an instigator" (2000, 174). As an average consumer of her country's culture, Mrs. Wheeler is the moral conscience that spurs her son to duty, helping to instill in Claude a reliance on idealism over practicality.

Like the whistling mother, Mrs. Wheeler is aware of the significance of her performance on Claude's last day at home; again, Derry Drake's words to Jean about the importance of "a memory for a man on the battlefield" resonate. This scene is one of few that is told from the point of view of someone other than Claude. Mrs. Wheeler comes to breakfast with the feeling that "she must acquit herself well" (Cather 1922, 212). Claude's avoidance of his mother on this last day hurts her, for it seems to suggest that he doubts her ability to "acquit herself well," an insult to his mother's strength. Their good-bye scene, however, is eerily reminiscent of that between Jack and his mother in *The Whistling Mother*:

> She rose, reaching toward him as he came up to her and caught her in his arms. She was smiling her little, curious intimate smile, with half-closed eyes.
>
> "Well, is it good-bye?" she murmured. She passed her hands over his shoulders, down his strong back and the close-fitting sides of his coat, as if she were taking the mould and measure of his mortal frame. Her chin came just to his breast pocket, and she rubbed it against the heavy cloth. Claude stood looking down at her without speaking a word. Suddenly his arms tightened and he almost crushed her.
>
> "Mother!" he whispered as he kissed her. He ran downstairs and out of the house without looking back. (214)

Claude's wife having refused the feminine role of savior and "Beautiful Soul," Mrs. Wheeler becomes the feminine presence for which the soldier fights and on which he relies for strength. His mother, like Jack's mother in *The Whistling Mother*, cannot abandon him. Although Claude spends his last morning at home with his father and brother, his very absence from his mother indicates the strength of their relationship, and Cather depicts only this good-bye scene, not Claude's leave-taking of his father and brothers.

The bond between mother and son continues and even intensifies as Claude approaches battle, reflecting the interdependency of the ideologies of home and of war. In France, Claude visits a church and feels "as if his mother were looking over his shoulder" (277). He wants to send her the names of his friend's violin recordings so that she will feel closer to him. And at the front he "wish[es] his mother could know how he felt this morning. But perhaps she did know. At any rate, she would not have him anywhere else" (294). Claude's relationship with his mother gives

him the spiritual strength to carry on with his idealism—with the belief
that he is fighting a just war and that he can earn glory through battle.
The emotional connection between them suggests that the structure of
the family and of domesticity underlies Claude's vision of war. The mother functions as the locus of the idealism that Claude relies on so heavily.
Rosowski points out that the women of One of Ours have a strong "adher-
ence to abstraction": both Mrs. Wheeler's and Enid's religious beliefs and
Mlle. Olive's patriotism (1986, 101). Women are supposed to hold these
ideals for the men; at the same time Claude becomes womanlike in devel-
oping his own spiritual beliefs about soldiers' shaping a new world.

At the end of the novel Mrs. Wheeler questions her son's idealism, but
she can do that questioning only after Claude's death and in a postwar
world. Significantly, the block between Claude and Mrs. Wheeler—that
is, her Christian faith—is replaced by Claude's idealism. Before the war
Claude feels separated from his mother by her belief in something that he
views with suspicion; one wonders if after the war, mother and son would
have been divided by Claude's unquestioning faith in the ideology of the
war. Mrs. Wheeler sees that the war has not erased the "flood of meanness
and greed" (Cather 1922, 370), and thus she knows that the idealism that
she has helped to create is false. She, unlike Claude, becomes disillusioned just as the returning soldiers are disillusioned, though she never
wavers in her faith in God.

Critics such as Rosowski and Gelfant argue that Claude leaves for the
war because he has no sense of family at home. In fact, the novel may be
indicting the very idea of the American family, rather than, as these critics imply, the Wheelers in particular. According to the propagandistic
relationship established in The Whistling Mother, Mrs. Wheeler has been
the "right" kind of mother, instilling her son with patriotism and holding
her head up at his departure for war; in this sense the Wheelers are a successful, functioning family. But Mrs. Wheeler's disillusionment with
American idealism at the end of the novel necessarily implies a corresponding disillusionment with the structure of the American family; the
intertwining of domestic ideology with war ideology demands that a questioning of one evoke a questioning of the other.

The family that demands heterosexuality of its children and inflicts
psychological damage on them through the sexual struggles of the parents
is the same family that creates a glorified vision of war. Cather draws
attention to this connection by returning, after Claude's death, to "the
banks of Lovely Creek, where it began" (369); "it" is Claude's story, a
story of a soldier that would be incomplete without the story of his
upbringing, family life, thwarted intellectual ambition, and failed marriage. The relationship of mother and son is one of the most deeply

explored issues in the novel; Claude and his mother have a close bond, yet it is a relationship burdened with social expectations about mothers and sons, sexual jealousy, and a gap created by differing spiritual beliefs. Cather's novel suggests that the socially inscribed roles of father, mother, and son create both young men who need to prove themselves through violence and also a neatly encapsulated idealism as a structure for them to understand the world and their own need for war.

Homosocial Incest in *A Son at the Front*

This sense of loss and meaninglessness resulting from the war is one of the reasons Wharton wrote her own postwar novel, A Son at the Front (1923). Many reviewers criticized Wharton for publishing a war novel "too late," when readers were tired of the war and wanted to move on; the *Bookman* critic claimed Wharton was still "too angry" over the war (quoted in Benstock 1995, viii). These reviews suggest that readers saw A Son at the Front primarily as a war propaganda novel. In fact Wharton had delayed the publishing of the novel and tried to market it as a study of French society during the war in order to appeal to a wider audience. Benstock shows that women critics were less antagonistic to the novel, pointing to Dorothea Lawrence Mann of the *Boston Evening Transcript*, who thought that Wharton portrayed well the feelings of soldiers' parents (ix). In addition, Judith Sensibar recently argued that A Son at the Front marks the "beginning of a revitalized and extraordinarily experimental late period" (1993, 244) in Wharton's career, suggesting that the novel signals Wharton's changing concerns and writing style.

Wharton's timing of her novel is closely connected to its meaning. In her autobiography, A Backward Glance, she writes that "I saw the years of the war, as I had lived them in Paris, with a new intensity of vision, in all their fantastic heights and depths of self-devotion and ardour, of pessimism, triviality and selfishness" (1964, 368). Alan Price points out that Wharton, heavily involved during the war in charity work, saw firsthand the corruption and selfishness the war brought out in people behind the lines (1996). Further, Wharton writes, "before I could settle down to this tale, before I could begin to deal objectively with the stored-up emotions of those years, I had to get away from the present altogether" (1964, 369); thus she suggests that the reason for the delay of the novel was her own need to distance herself from her story. Finally she explains that "although I had waited so long to begin it, the book was written in a white heat of emotion, and may perhaps live as a picture of that strange war-world of the rear, with its unnatural sharpness of outline and over-heightening of colour" (369). American readers and critics, after all, were not behind the lines in the sense that Wharton was; for them the "home front" was safe-ly delineated by an ocean, whereas Wharton lived within earshot of the fighting and was even one of the few women permitted to visit the front.

Within the text of *A Son at the Front* lie more reasons for Wharton's need to write the novel after the war. The main character, John Campton, is a painter whose son is a soldier; when he is able to think beyond his fear for his son's life, he views war through the eyes of an artist: "What a modeller of faces a great war must be! What would the people who came through it look like, he wondered" (Wharton 1923, 103). Wharton too may have wondered what changes the war would bring to those who lived through it; Benstock suggests that Wharton began reevaluating the character of her friends even while the war was going on (1994, 312). After seeing the cor-ruption and selfishness at the charities and in social circles, Campton muses whether the sacrifice of the young men is worth it. He concludes that "the efficacy of the sacrifice was always in proportion to the worth of the victims; and there at least his faith was sure" (Wharton 1923, 194). Wharton herself may have wished to show the corruption that under-mined the sacrifice and thus to redeem something from the waste. Finally, Campton longs for "a time . . . for art to interpret war; . . . the world in which men lived at present was one in which the word 'art' had lost its meaning" (128). Wharton may be suggesting that during war art is dimin-ished by the speculators who profit from it while men are dying; she may also be referring to a distinction between art and propaganda. During the war Wharton did write propaganda pieces, such as her book *Fighting France* (1919), and she may have felt that during war propaganda is a more appro-priate kind of writing. She felt the need to influence her readers, particu-larly Americans, to action. Wharton suggests that after the war, however, the job of writers and artists is to reflect, delve, and examine. Thus the tim-ing of the novel is directly related to its purpose: a reevaluation of war and society during wartime that can be understood only in hindsight.

A Son at the Front is the story of Campton, an American artist living in Paris, and his son George, who, due to his parents' "carelessness," was actually born in France. Divorced from George's mother, Campton unex-pectedly finds himself aligned with his former wife Julia and her second husband Anderson Brant in an attempt to keep George away from the front lines, on the "moral" grounds that George is only accidentally a French citizen and hence French soldier. Gradually Campton grows ashamed that his son is working a staff job rather than fighting a war that he comes to believe is justified and necessary for the preservation of Western civilization. Only when George is wounded do his parents dis-cover that he has secretly transferred to a fighting battalion. The novel follows Campton's desperate need to know his son, Campton's jealousy of and gradual reconciliation with George's wealthy stepfather, and the inevitable estrangement of George from his father. George's death after his second trip to the front leaves his father to work through and reconcile himself to the loss of his son.

Wharton's questioning of the idealized relationship between parents and sons in *The Whistling Mother* goes deeper than Cather's. Claude's parents never discourage him from fighting in the war. In *A Son at the Front*, however, Wharton gives prominence to a more realistic parental reaction. These parents are not the stoic, supportive parents of *The Whistling Mother*; they succumb to the emotions of fear and protectiveness. George's parents try everything in their power to keep him from the danger of the front lines. Only gradually does George's father come to desire that his son fight, and his mother never does. Even when Campton does come to feel the necessity of war, his doubts and fears prevent him from serving as a model for parental hawkishness.

Having "a son at the front" leaves the father with the complex problem of being the one to encourage the son to fight. Being the father of a soldier draws out contradictions in masculinity. As Julia taunts her ex-husband, "What do you suppose those young men out there think of their fathers, safe at home, who are too high-minded and conscientious to protect them?" (184) As a parent Campton should be protecting his son; as a man he sees the need for battle; and as a member of Western civilization he sees the need for the German threat to be removed. Thinking his son is working a safe desk job, Campton finds that the contradictions of his position leave him paralyzed:

> How could he say: "I'm satisfied; but I wish to God that George were not"? And was he satisfied, after all? And how could he define, or even be sure that he was actually experiencing, a feeling so contradictory that it seemed to be made up of anxiety of his son's safety, shame at that anxiety, shame at George's own complacent acceptance of his lot, and terror of a possible change in that lot? (214)

Campton fumbles with the unprecedented (for him) question of what a parent should feel about a son in relation to war; Wharton challenges the easy idealism of American propaganda.

In this novel Wharton shows a profound questioning of the tropes of World War I literature. Her novel is modernist in its isolated "hero" father and in the impact of Campton's consciousness on the narrative itself. Sensibar suggests that if we look beyond the consciousness of John Campton for a second narrator we see the irony behind the propagandistic battle cry (1993, 243–44). The presence of a narrator behind

Campton exposes the limits of consciousness and of storytelling even while attempting to reach beyond those limits. The reader knows, for example, that George is not at his safe desk job long before Campton does. Yet the clues from which the reader draws this conclusion are the same information available to Campton: family friend Adele Anthony's careful conversations with Campton; George's absence when his stepfather tries to visit him; George's "cold" letters. If the reader knows and Campton does not, it is only because the reader lacks Campton's blindness. At the same time, Campton recognizes his own blindnesses; that is, Campton is not so much blind as refusing to see. For example, he knows his refusal to "believe in the war" (Wharton 1923, 5) comes from his own intense desire to have the chance to travel with George (11). He resents that George has been supported by a stepfather but knows that if his son had lived with him, George would not have become who he is; recalling George's discovery of books, Campton acknowledges that "[i]f George had lived with him he might never have guessed the boy's latent hunger, for the need of books as part of one's daily food would scarcely have presented itself to him" (29–30). And Campton pointedly does not ask George's opinion of his relation to the war because of "the deadly fear of crystallizing his son's refusal" to be helped into a safe desk job (39). Campton's intentionally selective vision may be fundamental to his skill as an artist, but it hinders his ability to understand and interact meaningfully with other people.

Campton's willfully limited vision thus forces a continual reevaluation of the characters around him; once we understand that he sees what he wants to see, a narrative told from his point of view becomes suspect. Julia Brant, for example, is seen only through Campton's irritated interactions with her. Campton charges her with shallowness and selfishness; he thinks, "Her manner of loving their son was too different" (298). The reader must probe, however, to determine whether "different" means "wrong," as Campton implies. Campton seems to be saying that a mother's love is selfish, but through Campton's limited vision, Wharton critiques a gender system that leaves women with nothing to do but love their men. Campton has his art to broaden his mind or, if nothing else, to give him something to do, yet women in the novel cannot be artists and so have no role other than their relations to men. George's lover Madge Talkett, for example, mentions that she paints but refers to it as mere "dabbling." If Julia's love is selfish—and there is no evidence on which to make this judgment—Wharton also shows that Julia has been allowed no role other than mother and hostess.

Campton's contrast of paternal with maternal love seems to put the former on a higher, idealized plane and reduce the latter to mere animal instinct.[4] When Julia approaches her ex-husband in desperation to keep George at his staff job, Campton sees that "[i]f blind animal passion be the profoundest as well as the fiercest form of attachment, his love for his boy was at that moment as nothing to hers" (182). Campton, though previously as desperate as Julia to keep George from the fighting, now feels differently:

> The last four months had shown him man as a defenceless animal suddenly torn from his shell, stripped of all the interwoven tendrils of association, habit, background, daily ways and words, daily sights and sounds, and flung out of the human habitable world into naked ether, where nothing breathes or lives. That was what war did; that was why those who best understood it in all its farthest-reaching abomination willingly gave their lives to put an end to it. (183–84)

As an artist, Campton recognizes in humanity something above the animal passions, and he thus can no longer justify not fighting a war whose very purpose is to defend humanity's claim to civilization. Julia is never shown to have recognized this responsibility, and thus she remains to the reader lacking in intellectual capability. Yet when Campton tries to arrange for his son to convalesce at a rented apartment with him rather than at his mother's, Adele Anthony tells him to let George go to his mother "because it's natural—it's human. *You're* not always, you know" (317). Wharton's terms show her struggling with the biological aspects of motherhood and questioning her own definitions of human. Perhaps what Campton sees as "animal" love is more "human" than his own intense but isolated passion. Campton, after all, does not devalue a mother's love in general; his respect for the suffering of his landlady when she loses her son and his desire to draw her in her posture of suffering show he sees a nobility in maternal love, even if he must distance himself through art from that suffering.

Campton's relationship with Anderson Brant is even more complex than his relationship with Julia. Campton is jealous and resentful of Brant because of the other man's ability to do things for George, but with the onset of war he increasingly finds "a sense of their possessing a common ground of understanding that Campton had never found in his wife" (25). This common ground lies ironically in both men's experience of fatherhood. The text suggests in fact that Brant may have had a greater influence on George's character than Campton. For despite his prissiness and his crime—in Campton's eyes—of wealth, Brant is a generous and thoughtful man. Although Campton as an artist represents "Western civilization," it is Brant who provided young George with books, the very books from which George acquired the ideals that he leaves his desk job to fight for. Even though Campton at times despises Brant for his money and connections, he comes to accept what money and connections can do for George. He eventually realizes that he and Brant are remarkably similar; Campton's blind spots to the way the world works and to how people feel are paralleled in Brant by his failure to recognize that he has bought a forged painting.

The relationship of the two fathers never settles into an easy peace, but the tension between the men is itself significant. After George's death, Campton initially resists the Brants' appeals that he create a monument for his son. When he finally agrees to design the monument, the decision is in part for Brant, to give Brant the satisfaction of paying for it: "[I]t's going to cost a lot. . . . That's just what Brant'll like though, isn't it?" (424–25) Campton immediately repents of his "sneer": "I'll design it, and he shall pay for it. He'll want to—I understand that" (425). Here Campton recognizes that Brant gives through money as Campton gives through art. Sensibar calls Brant "the man [Campton] loves to hate" (1993, 252), a description appropriate for the dynamics of their relationship. Even though the two men have come to terms with each other, part of those terms includes jealous hostility. Their embattled relationship is itself a tribute to George, a monument to an ongoing love for the boy who is a product of them both.

Campton's tunnel vision also brings confusion to our understanding of George. Campton knows that he cannot see his son clearly: "He loved his son: yes—but he was beginning to see that he loved him for certain qualities he had read into him, and that perhaps after all—" (Wharton 1923, 176). Although Campton always believes the best about his son, we see hints that George manipulates his divorced parents. On his last night home George manages to go out with his friends and at the same time to avoid hurting his father's feelings by playing one parent off the other: "You see, it really wouldn't have done to tell mother that I was deserting her on my last evening because I was dining with you!" (93) Campton "felt ashamed of having failed to guess the boy's real motive," yet the "real motive" behind even this explanation is still hidden: George's rendezvous with his lover, something Campton never guesses but must be told. In contrast, there are moments of communion and knowledge between Campton and George that balance out Campton's willful blindnesses. At one point Campton starts to wonder about George's "moral balance" for not wanting to be in the war, finding it odd that his son has shown no anger at the sinking of the *Lusitania* (133), but we find later that in fact George has felt that anger. Campton's knowledge of his son is by no means completely wrong; often he is simply a half-step behind.

Yet Campton's fame as an artist originated in a painting of his son, suggesting something true and valuable in the relationship between artist and subject. Sensibar considers Campton's painting an "idealized image" (1993, 245) and it may be. But his portraits of other people indicate that Campton is not given to idealizing his subjects: He "made a success of [Adele Anthony's] long crooked pink-nosed face; but she didn't perceive it (she had wanted something oval, with tulle, and a rose in a taper hand)" (Wharton 1923, 46). Campton himself sees George's painting radiating a "communicative warmth" (58). If it is an idealized picture, the ideals the portrait represents are those common to society—the ideals, even, that George and the other young men in the novel head to the front to fight for. When Campton in a low moment wonders what is left to fight for, his friend Dastrey responds: "France . . . an Idea" (366). Campton recognizes the weight of this Idea even in the face of the threat to his son:

> An Idea: that was what France, ever since she had existed, had always been in the story of civilization; a luminous point about which striving visions and purpose could rally. And in that sense she had been as much Campton's spiritual home as Dastrey's. . . . If France went, western civilization went with her; and then all they had believed in and been guided by would perish. That was what George had felt; it was what had driven him from the Argonne to the Aisne. (366)

Although Cather's *One of Ours* ends with the failure of the ideals that drive Claude to France and even in *A Son at the Front* we see corruption and selfishness, Wharton, herself an artist nurtured by France, suggests that even if those ideals are not yet attained they cannot be forgotten.

Campton's limited vision and its effects on the reader give more impetus to the increasing critical tendency to include Wharton among the modernists. The text moves in two directions: toward an idealistic vision of the war as saving Western civilization (a move that brought the reviewers down on Wharton's head) and toward a questioning of those views. This dual movement is inherent in Campton's consciousness and in the narrative itself. Wharton aims at exposing the things that Campton knows but will not acknowledge just as she exposes what society knows and will not acknowledge. The locus of such hidden knowledge resides in the text as hints of incestuous feelings between father and son.

As Alan Price (1996) points out, much of Wharton's war and postwar writing focuses on incest, including *Summer* (1917), *The Mother's Recompense* (1925), and the "Beatrice Palmetto" fragment. Price speculates on possible reasons for this interest: leftover feelings from her affair with Morton Fullerton; a "general dislocation of values resulting from the war"; and the interest of two of Wharton's male friends in women who were considerably younger (173). Benstock speculates that Wharton's increased attention to sexuality and incest in her writing comes from learning that she herself may have been an illegitimate child (1994).[5] Kathy Fedorko, in *Gender and the Gothic in the Fiction of Edith Wharton*, argues that this focus on incest shows an "interest in sexual union as a fusion of conflicting yet related forces" (1995, 18). During the war years Wharton's interest in incest may have stemmed from the violence and conflict she saw around her and its relationship to art.

The homoerotics of *A Son at the Front* are less radical than they might seem. In "Edith Wharton as Propagandist and Novelist" Sensibar argues that *A Son at the Front* begins Wharton's exploration of "the ways in which social disruptions caused by World War I exposed and affected socially constructed notions of state, family, and masculinity and femininity. Particularly in the fiction she wrote during and after the war, she portrays masculinity as mutable and fluid" (1999, 165). Describing Wharton's earlier work *In Morocco* (1920) as a participation in and exposing of the connections between France's colonialism and homosexuality, Sensibar points out that Wharton's circle included a large number of homosexual or bisexual men (1999). Sensibar suggests that Wharton's own trip to Morocco, a prime vacation destination for gay men, led her to explore homoerotic terrain in *A Son at the Front* (165). Campton's initial plan is to travel in Africa with George for some time, suggesting Campton's thwarted homoerotic longing for his son.

Campton's relationship with his son is often described in physical terms. Just as Mrs. Wheeler holds her son in a final embrace, Campton's knowledge of his son seems to rest purely in the physical realm; when George was little, Campton remembers how "he could take him in his arms and make sure that he was the same Geordie, only bigger, browner, with thicker curlier hair, and tougher muscles under his jacket" (Wharton 1923, 284). The night before George leaves Campton gazes at his sleeping son with an eroticized eye toward the physical: "George lay on his side, one arm above his head, the other laxly stretched along the bed. He had thrown off the blankets, and the sheet, clinging to his body, modelled his slim flank and legs as he lay in dreamless rest" (53). Sensibar points to this passage as subversive of accepted gender conventions: "But rather than being directed toward a woman, and openly so, as men are meant to objectify women in this way, Campton's secret gaze is directed at, objectifies, and fetishizes another man" (1993, 249). Further, Sensibar argues, Campton's vision of his son lying as if dead on the battlefield undermines standard tropes of World War I literature:

> we see that by domesticating that convention [the "religio-erotic motif of the knight effigy"]—that is, by transferring it from battle front to home

front, from the trenches to the bedroom, and by changing it from the
paternal or fraternal comrade-in-arms relationship to the literally paternal father-son relation—Wharton probes behind the lines of one of the
most valorized relationships in the fiction and poetry of WWI. (250)

Although Sensibar is referring to the images in the poetry of Wilfred
Owen and other British war poets, Wharton's description of the
father/son relationship also subverts the accepted mother/son incest motif
in American literature.

Although war writing such as *The Whistling Mother* recognizes the
mother as the figure of creator aligned with the solider, Wharton points
out that the father is the locus of power in the gender system. This idea is
emphasized in *A Son at the Front*, where the father is an artist, a creator
in his own right. Several times in the novel Wharton parallels Campton's
creative power as artist with his creative power as father, such as when
Campton refers to George as "his own most beautiful creation" (1923,
176). Just as Campton frets over the ownership of his paintings and draw-
ings of George, he struggles as well to maintain "ownership" of his son—
the father and the artist combine as a creator/owner that rejects the
power of the role of the mother. Yet Campton does not have exclusive or
conscious power over George; the power of the father is limited by the
overwhelming power of society. Ultimately it is George's education in the
ideas of Western civilization that has the greatest effect on his character
and his actions. Campton himself, as an artist shaped by the intellectual
climate of France, is an unconscious source of the influences that will take
his son away from him. Although U.S. war propaganda relies on the
power of the mother, Wharton sees underneath to the patriarchal dynamics that ultimately shape sons *and* propaganda.

The hints of incest in *A Son at the Front* suggest a desire of the father,
emasculated by the war, to reclaim authority through the vitality of the
son. Fedorko, in her study, focuses specifically on male/female incest:
"Since . . . incest is destructive to women in Wharton's Gothic fiction,
her use of it seems instead to be a dramatization of the longing of a woman
to lose her sense of powerlessness by merging with the masculine power
that controls her" (1995, 18). In *A Son at the Front*, however, the sense of
powerlessness comes from the father's inability to fulfill a masculine role.
Campton sees himself "in white petticoats, with a long beard held on by
an elastic" (Wharton 1923, 190). Just as Jack in *The Whistling Mother*
takes his father's role as soldier, George usurps his father's role, both as soldier and as creator. Before the war Campton resigns himself to his son's
apparent lack of artistic instinct: "Apparently [George] was fated to be
only a delighted spectator and commentator; to enjoy and interpret, not

to create" (31). But by the end of the novel both George and his father recognize that George's job is to fight the war, and the ideological connection between soldiering and mothering suggest that in this way George has become a creator. George is a defender of Western civilization from the tyranny of violence, and, like Claude in *One of Ours*, who sees soldiers as birthing a new idea, George helps create a new world. That new world is partly limited to those young men who fight and die on the battlegrounds, but with his death George inspires a new artistic vision in his father, creating a new world forever marked by, but not limited to, the memory of violence and death.

The homoerotic relationship of father and son is based more deeply on the desire of the father to know the son, and this longing epitomizes the ultimate divide between individuals, a divide not created but thrown into high relief by the war. In *The Whistling Mother*, Jack's mother listens to him about the war "just exactly as another fellow would," thus proving herself the right sort of mother. In *A Son at the Front*, both son and parent are denied such a closeness, though to know his son is Campton's desperate, strongest desire. Benstock argues that the distance between the two is an inevitable result of the father's artistic vision: "[H]is sense of emotional separation from his son (a distance that widens as the story progresses) mirrors an aspect of the novel's artistic theme: to capture his subject, the painter requires distance and perspective. The longing for paternal intimacy with his son is tempered by Campton's stronger desire to turn his son into art—to memorialize him" (1995, xii). Art must distance itself from war, both in emotion, time, and space—hence Wharton's own need to wait before writing *A Son at the Front*.

Yet Wharton also suggests that there is a deeper cultural gap between father and son. George, using a "we" that includes other young men of his generation and excludes his father, initially claims: "People are too healthy and well-fed now; they're not going off to die in a ditch to oblige anybody" (Wharton 1923, 32). George's terms change, however, when Germany invades Belgium: "The howling blackguards! The brigands! This isn't war—it's simple murder!" (90). George comes to feel the need to defend Western civilization, and in this change in attitude he aligns himself further with a new generation of men, separated from their fathers by ideas. Campton himself, with one of his odd shots in the dark, attempts to save his son from "the consequences of his parents' stupid blunder" (77); Campton's immediate reference is to George's birth in France, but his words seem also to refer to the historical events that have led to the moment of war. He can save his son from neither, and he can only sense the gap that divides the generations.

Fighting on the front lines, George becomes further separated from his father by the horrors of his experience. Witnessing and participating in the fighting has created a part of George that his father cannot access; watching George with Mme. Lebel after the loss of her son Campton sees "[t]hese two are closer to each other than George and I, because they've both seen the horror face to face. He knows what to say to her ever so much better than he knows what to say to his mother or me" (375). It is the parents' lack of experience that permanently divides them from the sons. As Benstock argues, "For Campton (as for Edith Wharton), the war represents a great divide within history and between human beings—between those who experienced the unspeakable at first hand and those who did not" (1995, xiv). The war transforms George in the eyes of those around him. George's friend Boylston sees this as clearly as Campton does, saying of George that he is "[t]ransfigured, say; no, trans—what's the word in the theology books? A new substance . . . somehow . . ." (Wharton 1923, 390). The word Boylston seems to be searching for is "transubstantiated"; the war has become a spiritual experience that affects the physical realm.

The "unbridgeable abyss" between father and son is made insurmountable by the inability to communicate. George cannot speak of the war, for its horrors cannot be contained in language; for this reason Wharton never describes the front or the fighting, leaving them to the reader's incomprehension as they are to Campton's. Lying in his hospital bed, George looks at his father "with eyes as void of experience [as a baby], or at least of any means of conveying it" (292). The problem of communication is larger than the war; it is fundamental to language itself. The very phrase "a son in the war" is heavy with incomprehensible meaning for Campton: "What did it mean, and what must it feel like, for parents in this safe denationalized modern world to be suddenly saying to each other with white lips: A son in the war?" (70) Campton's struggle to understand these words epitomizes his reaction to the war. Language fails him; the words are meaningless without experience to back them up. When George announces to his father that he is after all returning to the front, "Campton said—or imagined he said: 'I see—I do see, already—' though afterward he was not even sure that he had spoken" (379). Campton's artistic vision makes necessary that he literally see things before understanding them, and so understanding things that cannot be seen is almost impossibly difficult for him. Here, by saying he "sees," Campton means to express his understanding of his son's need to return, yet the possibility that he does not even speak these words shows the problem of communication. He has moments in which he has brief glimpses of George's soul and feels they have touched each other, but he cannot ever be sure. George's death epitomizes the difficulty of ever truly communicating with another's innermost self.

Wharton suggests that incestuous desire is closely related to the violence into which Europe is thrust by the First World War. In "Civilization and Its Discontents," Freud argues that "it is impossible to overlook the extent to which civilization is built upon a renunciation of instinct, how much it pre-supposes precisely the non-satisfaction (by suppression, repression or some other means?) of powerful instincts. This 'cultural frustration' dominates the large field of social relationships between human beings. As we already know, it is the cause of the hostility against which all civilizations have to struggle" (1985, 286–87). Campton's sexual longing for his own son is one of the instincts that is suppressed in order for the creation of civilization to occur. As these instincts remain trapped and shut away, the pressure builds; in this way is Campton implicated in the violence that consumes his son. George fights an external battle in the name of protecting a civilization that rests on internal battles.

Conclusion

Both *One of Ours* and *A Son at the Front* suggest that the violence of the Oedipal triangle—the structure of the family—is the locus of inherent violent underpinnings in Western civilization. Relationships within the domestic sphere thus become fundamental to power struggles and ideological investments in the public world, and both Cather and Wharton describe incestuous desire as a source and symbol of the violence of war. These texts interrogate the structure of the American family, as this family creates ideology that is unreliable and is built through an underlying violence that makes the violence of war acceptable, even desirable. Interestingly, these two childless women expose such problems in a subtle but pointed way, although both fail to imagine an alternate family structure.

By picking up on the gap between parents and sons, men and women, soldiers and noncombatants, Cather and Wharton show themselves as modernist writers. The gap that seems contextualized within the context of war becomes blown open by war, and, although the First World War is not the lone cause of modernism, its ideals and its violence led to a reevaluation of the self and the individual's relationships to others and to society as a whole. Male writers—both those who experienced the war and those who did not—positioned themselves as experts on this new view of life from the perspective of the inside. Whereas Wharton's John Campton struggles from his side of the gap to see who his son is, other writers create characters who speak from the side of the soldier.

Chapter 3
Domesticity at the Front:
Gender, Resistance, and Self

Novels that explore the soldier's experience in the First World War often show disillusionment with the ideals and attitudes of the home and a sense of disjunction within the self. Whereas sentimental and domestic novels inscribe the soldier's ideal role, war novels often explode that role, exposing the idealization with which noncombatants view war. War novels show the hollowness of war ideology, yet in many cases they also rely on similar literary strategies as do more sentimental works: Descriptions of domestic activities and rituals are often included in war novels, and the presence of these details can help us understand the soldier's changing relationship toward the home and also his need for these rituals. The First World War was fought in terms of a battle for civilization; the inclusion— or exclusion—of domestic ritual reveals attitudes toward and characteristics of the civilization soldiers fought to preserve.

To look for the significance of domesticity in war novels may seem contradictory. The war plot emphasizes that soldiers have been removed from their homes and must make do for themselves; activities such as cooking, eating, sleeping, and nursing all appear to be basic, subsistence acts. But the inclusion of these details can be revealing. In arguing for the reevaluation of previously disregarded works by women, Kolodny claims the right to reread texts in light of new ideas: "All the feminist is asserting, then, is her own equivalent right to liberate new (and perhaps different) significances from these same texts; and at the same time, her right to choose which features of a text she takes as relevant because she is, after all, asking new and different questions of it" (1985a, 160). As Romines argues, women's domestic writing highlights activities that have previously gone unseen and been taken for granted (1992). If it has become appropriate to reevaluate the work of women writers with the understanding that meaning can be found in "invisible" details, it also becomes appropriate to reevaluate—to ask new and different questions of—the writing of male writers, whose works take domestic activities for granted yet cannot seem to leave them out entirely.

Figure 4. "For Your Boy." Photograph courtesy of the Archives and Special
Collections, University of Nebraska-Lincoln Libraries

In the war novels this chapter discusses, descriptions of domestic rituals and arrangements suggest a subversion of established gender roles. In
the texts, food, shelter, and domestic ritual play subtle but significant
roles; the authors describe what the soldiers eat, where they sleep, and how
they relate to each other. These details show men taking on traditionally
female roles; one propaganda poster shows a YMCA worker serving coffee to "your boy," performing the mother's work of caring for her son.

It therefore becomes apparent that if these soldiers can make a world without women, then the gender system that divides war from domestic ideologies becomes suspect—that is, it becomes more apparent that gender and gender roles are constructed, not inherent. At the same time, the soldiers' comfort in this all-male world reinforces the division between the sexes. The soldiers eventually come to understand that they have more in common with each other and even with enemy soldiers than they do with noncombatants at home; women, who are not part of the military family, are necessarily excluded from the common consciousness and communion of soldiers. Thus the difference between the sexes is shown to be arbitrary even while the gulf between them is widened by the soldiers' experience of war.

This experience of war undermines soldiers' understanding of the principles on which they have been taught civilization is based. Domesticity in normal times implies and often relies on a context of affection and peacefulness; during war, however, domestic activities take place amid violence and chaos. This disjunction emphasizes society's inability to prepare soldiers for the event of war. Elaine Scarry's *Body in Pain: The Making and Unmaking of the World* probes the underlying principles of war: The activity of war is injuring the enemy, but this injuring is not in itself the determining factor of a winner (1985). The structure of war "requires both the reciprocal infliction of massive injury and the eventual disowning of the injury so that its attributes can be transferred elsewhere, as they cannot if they are permitted to cling to the original site of the wound, the human body" (64). Injury to bodies helps determine who wins the war, but the actual marks left on the bodies do not indicate who the winner is—only that a war took place. To understand this idea, Scarry explains, we must recognize the body as fundamentally political, with its learned behaviors marking it as American, German, French, and so on. A soldier, by agreeing to kill, "wrench[es] around his most fundamental sanctions about how within civilization (and this particular civilization, his country) another embodied person can be touched; he divests himself of civilization, decivilizes himself" (122). At the same time, war is essential to a country's definition of itself. Hence, the violence of war is fundamental to the "unmaking" and "making" of civilization.

Scarry's idea of war has several implications for the individual soldier. He must act against his ingrained belief that to kill is wrong—a belief taught him by the very civilization that he now defends. By fighting and killing, he alienates himself from the home for which he fights. Much of the writing about the First World War shows an increasing revulsion against both killing and society; the soldier finds that he can no longer support the society he has believed in, but often he continues to fight anyway. These contradictory impulses inflict severe psychological damage on soldiers, who are forced to negotiate the complexities of war and home, reality and ideology. In *No Man's Land: Combat and Identity in World War I*, Eric J. Leed comments that during war the soldier learns that instead of there being two worlds, one of peace and a separate one where violence is permitted, "there is *only* an industrial world, the reality of which defined them in war much more than it had in peace. In the trenches men learned that mechanized destruction and industrial production were mirror images of each other" (1979, 194). That is, even though soldiers may have approached war by pretending that such violence takes place in a context sharply delineated from the world of peace, they learn that in fact no such division exists.

Writing about war can be as problematic as fighting the war. Writing, like domestic ritual, is a sign of civilization; when a soldier writes about war, he attempts to process a civilization-destroying activity into something that can be understood by civilization—by his audience, most of whom have never fought in a war, and also by himself. In their introduction to *The Violence of Representation: Literature and the History of Violence* Nancy Armstrong and Leonard Tennenhouse argue that writing can be "not so much about violence as a form of violence in its own right" (1989, 2). That is, the ability to read and write makes possible the exclusion of those who cannot represent themselves; thus, Otherness becomes a vast category for all forms of difference. The dynamics of difference necessarily require that the self can never be fully explained in words (7). The relationship between Wharton's George Campton and his father, for example, epitomizes the violence of self-definition that precludes a true communion with another person; war does not create but rather highlights this problem. The difficulty, as Evelyn Cobley argues in her book *Representing War*, is that writing about the First World War is an impossible task to begin with; the war defied everything the soldiers knew about war, but they had no way to express their experiences except through literary forms already established, forms that, instead of resisting and challenging social norms, "reproduce . . . the ideological values against which they are being mobilized" (1993, 10). For the soldier to write, he must negotiate a process that commits further violence—intended violence against given ideological structures and literary forms and unintentional violence against his experiences and his sense of himself.

The problem is complicated by the gendering of war and power. As Armstrong and Tennenhouse argue, the dynamics of difference always become subsumed as gendered positions: the dominant masculine and the submissive feminine (1989). But soldiers of the First World War did not feel themselves dominant; the enforced passivity of the trenches and the paralysis of mechanized warfare stripped them of a sense of having control over their lives. Leed identifies "the defensive personality," originating specifically with trench warfare (1979, 197). Coming from an ideological context in which women function as "Beautiful Souls," soldiers felt themselves further disempowered; Armstrong and Tennenhouse point out that often the subtle power of mothers is dominant, "the power of normative culture" that is itself a form of violence (1989, 4). The civilization for which soldiers went forth to fight had been inscribed and instilled by the mothers. The soldier becomes doubly submissive to the war and to a feminine culture.

The war novels discussed here show that male soldiers have a complicated relationship to gender and thus to the domestic world. If writing is itself a form of violence, then writing about war is doubly violent, and we must ask on whose and with whose bodies this violence is enacted. The violence of war on male and female bodies is represented differently, yet during conflict, male soldiers may find themselves in feminized positions. If, as Armstrong and Tennenhouse suggest, Otherness is a "negation of self" (16)—a category containing all of the things that the self is not—what happens when the self, the white male soldier, becomes negated by the mass destruction of war? The soldier becomes in effect the housewife, an individual with control over only small, daily tasks but with no control over his own body, married to the larger machine of war and subject to the whims of the enemy and even of his own, often invisible, superiors.

For this chapter it is useful to look first at the last part of Cather's *One of Ours* (1922), which takes place in the male world of the French front, and examine the domesticity integrated with the novel's military action. *One of Ours* is particularly relevant here, as we see a work that begins as a domestic novel infused with an ideology of war and gender and becomes, in its later parts, a war novel that remains focused on domesticity. After *One of Ours* I move to works by two male authors who experienced the war: Thomas Boyd's *Through the Wheat* (1923) and John Dos Passos's *One Man's Initiation: 1917* (1920) and *Three Soldiers* (1921). These novels all describe soldiers' experiences at the front in France and in a world limited almost exclusively to men, but they also include descriptions of domestic activities. These domestic details reveal a disillusionment with the ideology of the home front but also show a need for the comfort and security domesticity can provide.

Claude Wheeler's Gender Crossing

Including Cather among these male war writers brings up the critical difficulty of a woman's writing about the exclusively male experience of being a soldier in the First World War. Certainly Hemingway, the alpha male of war writers, felt Cather's Pulitzer-prize-winning *One of Ours* to be

inaccurate and fanciful. Yet Hemingway's later comment about Stephen
Crane in the introduction to his 1955 edited collection *Men at War*
undercuts his discounting of Cather:

> Crane wrote [*The Red Badge of Courage*] before he had ever seen any war.
> But he had read the contemporary accounts, had heard the old soldiers,
> they were not so old then, talk, and above all he had seen Matthew Brady's
> wonderful photographs. Creating his story out of this material he wrote
> that great boys' dream of war that was to be truer to how war is than any
> war the boy who wrote it would ever live to see. It is one of the finest books
> of our literature. It is as much of one piece as a great poem is. (1968, 10)[1]

As Michael Reynolds shows in *Hemingway's First War*, Hemingway wrote
In Our Time and *A Farewell to Arms* just as Crane wrote *The Red Badge of
Courage*: drawing on newspaper articles, stories from former soldiers, and
photographs (1976, 11–13). And this is also the method Cather used to
write *One of Ours*. She read letters from her cousin Grosvenor Cather to
his mother, read other soldiers' letters, invited former soldiers to her New
York apartment to tell her their stories, and traveled to France (Rosowski
1986, 95).

Janis Stout offers another interpretation of male critics' rejection of
One of Ours: "[Cather] had shown the soldier himself as deluded and the
women who surround him as being more knowing than he. Perhaps these
male powers of the literary world preferred to see the male soldiers, not
their women, as the perceptive ones, able to see and judge the bankrupt-
cy of outworn notions" (2000, 180). Having a woman, ideologically
aligned with the normative culture, instead of endorsing that culture
exposing its corruption threatens the only privileged position a soldier
could salvage from the emasculating First World War.

In fact, *One of Ours* provides an important bridge between domesticity and war; it shows literally how a domestic novel can become a war
novel, yet the parts that are about the home and the parts that are about
the war feed into each other. The first sections of the novel show domestic rituals and their function and ways in which the war is incorporated
into and defined by domesticity, and the last part shows Claude as a soldier but also as a man highly attuned to domestic nuances. The "Voyage
of the *Anchises*" section of the novel functions as a transitional space,
both for Claude and for the novel itself. Claude is in a military world, but
there is no battle, only the daily functions of life and the crisis of disease
and death—both events that call for a domestic response. The novel is
both a domestic novel and a war novel, signifying that barriers dividing
these novel forms are more arbitrary than they may seem.

As discussed in chapter 1, Claude finds in the military a sense of belonging that he does not feel at home. As critics Rosowski and Yongue argue, Claude replaces his biological family with a military family. Although Claude resists the traditional heterosexual family structure (on the voyage to France Claude enjoys "the happy feeling that he was the least married man on the boat" [Cather 1922, 247]), the war gives him a purpose for his energy and provides a structure in which he has a clearly defined place. After being on leave, for example, Claude and his friend Hicks begin "to feel cheerful at getting back to their chums and their own little group" (319). D. A. Boxwell argues that *One of Ours* shows the complex male dynamics underlying war: The novel "reveals a profound awareness of male homosocial desire as a motivation for war, but also the problematic nature of that desire in war" (1994, 290). That is, homosocial desire must be and is continually contained and renamed within a military context. The military-as-family feeling allows men to create bonds with each other while excluding sexual overtones.

Part of Claude's enjoyment of being in the military is the absence of women, since consequently he is free to act in traditionally female roles. Rosowski argues that Claude actually wants to live like a woman, "to give himself up to something more powerful than himself" (1986, 110). She also points out that Claude is "most himself when he is most domestic" (111). On the ship Claude willingly nurses other soldiers, and he finds the "effeminate" wristwatch "a very useful article" (Cather 1922, 241). In addition to nursing, he assumes a parental function. When one of his soldiers is "snivelling and crying like a baby," Claude disciplines him not as his own father would, with ridicule and humiliation, but with kindness and understanding. This disciplinary action combines maternal and paternal roles; the paternal authority is carried out with a maternal care: "You're scared, that's all. Now drink this tea" (239). Thus Claude is able to eliminate differences in gender roles in a single-sex setting—not in favor of the feminine, but in favor of gender neutrality.

At the front Claude still shows a desire for homeyness and domesticity, just as he did when courting Enid. The novel shows him moving back and forth between the front lines and the security of French homes. He appreciates the luxuries of the Joubert household, where he is quartered when he first comes to France: "[I]t was good to lie again in a house that was cared for by women" (282). Later, on leave from the front, he finds "perfect bliss" (326) as he gets into bed. But this domesticity is more of a treat for Claude than it is a place of permanence; at the Fleurys' house Claude wants to run because of "something agreeable" in the daily rhythms of the home (335). He has come to prefer the male society of the military, and he has even found satisfaction in domesticity at the front.

The dugout in which he and his friend David Gerhardt are quartered is described in detail:

> There were two bunks nailed against the side walls,—wooden frames with wire netting over them, covered with dry sandbags. Between the two bunks was a soap-box table, with a candle stuck in a green bottle, an alcohol stove, a *bain-marie*, and two tin cups. On the wall were coloured pictures from *Jugend*, taken out of some Hun trench. (294–95)

Calling the space a "comfortable little hole," Claude appreciates it despite its barrenness (295). There is even a sense of peace and domestic harmony with the enemy: "Here and there thin columns of smoke began to rise; the Hun was getting breakfast; everything was comfortable and natural" (293). The front itself becomes a space for Claude's emotional home.

Like the first parts of the novel, the section about Claude's experience in France is filled with descriptions of eating and housekeeping. What Claude considers "[t]he bravest act of his life" (262) is speaking French to a woman in order to buy cheese for his men. The novel thus suggests that negotiating a new culture is as daunting as facing a war—especially for Claude, who always notices domestic details. He looks with distaste at the dirty hotel room where the aviator Victor receives him:

> The heavy red cotton-brocade hangings and lace curtains were stiff with dust, the thick carpet was strewn with cigarette-ends and matches. Razor blades and "Khaki Comfort" boxes lay about on the dresser, and former occupants had left their autographs in the dust on the table. Officers slept there, and went away, and other officers arrived,—and the room remained the same, like a wood in which travellers camp for the night. (266)

Thus the war has conflated home-front and battle-front spaces, for the metaphorical "wood" through which "travellers" pass will soon be the forest in which soldiers sleep. Claude also carefully notes the details of the home of Mlle. Olive, including the "coloured war posters on the clean board walls, brass shell-cases full of wild flowers and garden flowers, canvas camp-chairs, a shelf of books, a table covered by a white silk shawl embroidered with big butterflies" (310). At the front, in comparison, the men are conscious of their wet clothing and their inadequate food, a "dry biscuit at noon" (356).

Even though casually mentioned as necessary accompaniments to the story, domestic elements such as food or clothing are neither neutral nor insignificant. Usually domestic details signify Claude's desire for comfort and belonging, but occasionally they take on aspects of danger. On a march toward the front, Claude fails to notice a lit match, which the enemy uses as a target. The damage report after the subsequent attack includes the deaths of two lieutenants hit by a shell and "Captain Owens, he near got scalded with the stew" (358). The incidental inclusion of spilled stew with enemy shells in the damage report suggests the way in which the domestic has been accepted as part of front-line life. Later, a supply train brings much-needed "ammunition and coffee" (364) to the troops at the front, erasing the distinction between war supplies and domestic supplies. The domestic can be comforting or dangerous, but it cannot be taken for granted.

Despite Claude's ability to see the comfortable and the familiar even at the front, evidence of rottenness keeps turning up. War, as Mahailey and Claude's mother have imagined, is depicted as a disruption of domesticity. The tired French woman trying to nurse the German baby brings this point home to Claude: The evidence of rape and of the mixing of German blood into a French family shows war infiltrating domesticity. Even the soldiers' domestic spaces are violated. The soldiers bathe in a shell hole filled with water, only to discover that a dead body lies at the bottom; they have washed themselves with water contaminated by death and decay. In the trench where Claude's last battle takes place, the engineers manage to clear out or bury most of the bodies, but one hand refuses to stay covered: It continually reminds the men of the death on which they stand.

These grotesque intrusions into Claude's domestic world reflect his recurring feeling of homelessness and displacement. He enjoys France, which has reminders of home in the cottonwoods but which also has the allure of the "Old World." Yet he never feels confident that his presence is truly wanted: "Since he had come back [to the Jouberts], Claude had more than once wondered whether he took too much for granted and felt more at home here than he had any right to feel" (327). He worries that he cannot distinguish manners from feeling, ritual from true appreciation. He defends his presence to himself, thinking, "anyway, he wasn't a tourist. He was here on legitimate business" (327), transforming the private world of the domestic that he has found in the military into the public world of "business." In this way he repeats the nineteenth-century attitude of treating the "home" as a public space; in both cases the domestic world—the home or the military—serves as a means for disseminating public virtue.

Claude does not allow these doubts to weaken his idealism, and the genderless world he creates becomes integral to his vision. By eliminating gender roles, soldiers appropriate as well the ability to give birth. David Gerhardt, speculating on the unknowable causes and consequences of the war, says to Claude, "when the sons of the gods were born, the mothers always died in agony. . . . I've sometimes wondered whether the young men of our time had to die to bring a new idea into the world" (330). Claude's idealism is one of the reasons Cather was criticized for *One of Ours*, yet, as Rosowski points out, Claude's ideals are all proven to be empty by the text itself (1986, 106–7). The soldiers become mothers, but what they give birth to is something dark and monstrous. Claude's mother is glad that he does not return to see how futile his efforts have been. Cather, after exposing the arbitrary nature of gender roles and the importance of domestic activities even in an all-male world, then leaves ambiguous the results of such gender crossing.

For the nature of violence makes such attempts self-defeating. Armstrong and Tennenhouse refer to the violence of gender: "[T]he only gender that can presume to speak as if ungendered and for all genders is the dominant gender" (1989, 3). Even though Claude may strive to shed his masculinity and live in a world where gender does not exist, such an endeavor does violence to the normative culture. Claude—and Cather— are caught in a self-perpetuating loop defined by the nature of violence itself. War, historically defined, demands the presence of only men, even if those men perform women's roles. And the act of representation, itself an act of violence, assumes a masculine authority to speak. Claude may feel at home in a world without clearly defined gender roles, but that world exists only because those assumptions about gender roles have eliminated women from both the military and the space of war.

Boyd and the Soldier's Psychological Rebellion

Whereas Cather uses ironic distance to portray disillusionment with the ideological premises of World War I, other war novelists employ more direct strategies for showing the soldiers' disenchantment with American ideals and the disintegration of their sense of self in the face of technological warfare. Thomas Boyd's 1923 novel *Through the Wheat* describes the psychological damage of the First World War on one American soldier. Critic Stanley Cooperman categorizes William Hicks as a "spiritual sleepwalker" (1967, 59) or "psychological corpse" (62), referring to Hicks's eventual numbness to the world around him. The novel follows Hicks through several battles, his experiences at the front and on leave, and his interactions with his fellow soldiers. The novel ends with Hicks walking back to the front to retrieve the rifle he had thrown away, seemingly unresponsive and invulnerable to the oncoming German soldiers and their bullets.

Soldiers in *Through the Wheat* have an apparently unconflicted relation-ship with the home and the home front. Hicks, concerned that he is in trouble for falling asleep during his watch, wonders how his mother and his girl will react if he gets court-martialed; he worries about maintaining their good opinion. Mail call is a ceremony, a handing out of letters like presents at Christmas. The news is not always good; one soldier gets a "Dear John" letter and subsequently shoots himself in the foot, but all of the soldiers look forward to any connection to home. But letters taper off as the novel progresses, reflecting the soldiers' increasing emotional isolation.

Hicks, however, has received a rather unusual letter from his mother. She offers to send him cyanide of potassium for use in case he is gassed. His mother understands that this war is different from previous wars: "You know, son, . . . this war is not like the war that grandpapa used to tell you about. Those frightful Germans have liquid fire and deadly gases, and it is only when I think of how you would suffer if you were burned by their infernal liquid fire that I offer to send it" (Boyd 1923, 101). She proposes a code, that he mark his letter with a cross if he wants the cyanide. Her letter reveals an understanding of the war that is seldom shown by noncombatants in writings about the First World War. Hicks refuses the offer for fear of purgatory—a religious sensibility that probably came from his mother herself. As the locus and instiller of cultural and religious values, Hicks's mother has made her own offer impossible to accept. And unlike other mothers, especially the idealized "whistling mother," Hicks's mother cries when he goes off to training camp, displaying what he considers unpatriotic feeling. Home is a comfort, yet it is laced with the strength of a mother's love—and its brutal practicality—that would send her son the means to kill himself.

Like *One of Ours*, *Through the Wheat* describes the soldiers' lives in terms of daily rituals. These rituals are a necessary means of getting through the war; in order to function, soldiers' minds must be directed away from continual thoughts of danger and violence: "The platoon plodded along, their thoughts too taken up with the matter at hand—arriving at their quarters, being fed, and going to sleep—to give further thought to the eventuality of their being killed" (57). At the front, even afternoon bombardments become part of the daily routine: "Between the time when an attack might be expected and the diurnal four-o'-clock German bombardment, the moment gave the platoon a chance once more to assume their normal existence" (143).[2] Their "normal existence" includes getting out of the trench and spending some time reflecting, time that helps them hold on to their feelings of humanity. When they are relieved from the trenches they establish other routines:

> They drilled four hours a day, were inspected daily by the acting company commander, tried to rid themselves of lice by swimming in the Marne,[3]

made secret expeditions to neighboring villages, . . . cursed their officers, and tried to scare the new men by exaggerating the frightfulness of the front, [and] gorged themselves on the plentiful rations. (168)

Although not all of the preceding activities are necessarily domestic rituals, they do fit Romines's definition, part of which includes "a 'dramatic' group-making quality" (1992, 12). The communal experiences in *Through the Wheat* help build bonds among the soldiers. For Hicks and Pugh, for example, the rituals of daily life result in a close friendship, so close that when Hicks watches Pugh be killed while trying to crawl to shelter, "[h]e felt himself, with Pugh, striving to attain shelter behind the absurd little mound. It was his hand that reached out to touch it!" (Boyd 1923, 245)

In the novel, food and eating, inherent parts of domestic ritual, are often described in detail, with two big feasts serving as counterbalances to the action of battle. The first feast occurs when the men find an empty town with chickens, potatoes, and wine still remaining. The soldiers prepare a huge meal, more than they can eat, and then sit down at a large table, set with a linen tablecloth and "china plates and silver knives and forks." As the soldiers luxuriate in good food, this meal becomes "a religious ceremony" (69). Hicks, however, points out the irony that they are eating the chickens of the people whose homes they came to Europe to save; like Claude Wheeler, he worries about the soldiers' making themselves too much at home. These novels suggest that even though the comfort of domesticity is to be desired for the soldiers' emotional well-being, on the other hand such comfort prevents them from doing their job. The second feast takes place after the men have returned from the front, and the smell of fried steak reminds one of the soldiers of being at home. Ironically, however, the food also reminds the men of the events of the battle: "[T]he quantity had been prepared for sixty men, while there were only fourteen men to dine" (164). Thus descriptions of food inherently bring new meaning to the act of eating itself. The pleasure of both feasts is undercut by the implications behind them, of disruption, destruction, and death.

The food degenerates in quality as the soldiers move toward the front. There the men eat "cold boiled potatoes, cold coffee, and black French bread"—food that is itself treacherous, as one soldier remarks, because too many potatoes can cause cold sores (87). In less fortunate times in the trenches, the men open cans of beef: "[T]he contents would be exposed, green and sepulchrally white, the odor mingling and not quite immersed in the odor of decaying human flesh" (133). The meat becomes symbolically equivalent to dead bodies, forcing the soldiers into a kind of cannibalism of their fellow soldiers and suggestive of the internal corruption in the U.S. military itself. Such mixing of meat and corpses also suggests Christ's sacrifice, but the eating of the flesh of the sacrificed soldiers offers only memory, not redemption. The decreasing quality of the food reflects the emotional decay the men face as they fight: "Their three weeks' experience in the woods had so bludgeoned their senses that they had been unresponsive when told that they were to be relieved. But after a while they partly recovered under the stimulation of the picture of warm food and a shelter of comparative safety" (161). Food and shelter foster the quality of being human.

For if it is ritual that gives meaning to human lives, war is the destroyer of ritual and thus the destroyer of humanity. The war is represented as increasingly absurd, and this absurdity comes from the increasing encroachment of violence into supposedly protected spaces. Part of this absurdity comes from the incompetence of the officers and military strategists, whom the novel harshly mocks; one soldier, for example, is killed by his own army because an officer "forgot" about the raiding party in the no-man's land between the trenches. Recognizing the incompetence and corruption in the military, Hicks has accepted them as the way things are. But after being relieved from the trenches and taking rest in the woods, one soldier is killed by a tree branch falling on his head. For Hicks, "the treachery, the unexpectedness of the calamity" is the turning point in his attitude toward the war:

> He would be at hand for as many attacks as general headquarters could devise; he would do his part in advancing the Allied cause; he would help save the world for democracy; he would make war to end war; he would tolerate Y. M. C. A. secretaries; he would go without food, clothing and sleep—so he told the officers—but he would not return to the woods. . . . For him, he felt, life had ended, the world had come to a full stop. (211)

The use of the propagandistic phrases shows Hicks's awareness of the hollowness of those very phrases; Hicks recognizes what Scarry shows to be the discrepancy between war's purpose ("saving the world for democracy") and its activity: injuring (1985). The soldier killed by the falling branch is just as dead as if he had been shot by the Germans, and Hicks is vividly reminded that death has no relation to his nation's stated goals.

His world continues to disintegrate, as he becomes increasingly separated from reality. He is, as Cooperman says, a good soldier (1967, 163); he is competent and even seems to have an unnatural ability to walk through machine gun fire unharmed. Being a "good soldier" is the most unique thing about him. He is not ambitious (like Dan Fuselli), not a leader (like Claude Wheeler), not educated (like Claude, Dick Gephardt, and John Andrews), and not an ambulance driver (like Martin Howe and Frederic Henry). But being a good soldier means that Hicks becomes lost in the world of the violence; he talks to dead soldiers, and "a day's occupation" becomes killing Germans lurking behind almost every bush (Boyd 1923, 261). At the end of the novel, he returns to the front to find a gun that he had thrown away, indicating his continued commitment to an army and an endeavor he can no longer understand or respect. Caught in technological warfare, Hicks has become a mechanized soldier, at an extreme psychological and emotional cost.

Thus *Through the Wheat* suggests that war necessarily includes domesticity and that domesticity includes violence. Domestic rituals provide meaning, but that meaning reflects the eroding of "civilized" principles. Domesticity cannot save the soldier from the psychological horrors he must face; rather, domesticity becomes a sign of those same horrors. The feasts suggest violence and death, and home reminds Hicks of the danger he faces. Unable to escape the ideological paradigm forced upon him by the military as well as the home, Hicks does his job and loses his mind.

Domesticity and Violence: Dos Passos's World of the Absurd

Like many young men, John Dos Passos had a conflicted attitude toward the First World War. The war provided an opportunity to learn new things and experience the world, but at the same time it made indelible the brutality and stupidity of humanity. Dos Passos had lived abroad as a child and toured Europe several times before the war broke out, and he came to think of Europe as a cultural home. When the fighting started he looked for a way to get involved. He felt drawn to the war: In 1916 he wrote his friend Walter Rumsey Marvin that "there is something frightfully paralyzing to me in the war. Everything I do, everything I write seems so cheap and futile— If Europe is to senselessly destroy itself—It's as if a crevasse had opened and all the fair things, all the mellow, all the things that were to teach us in America how to live, were slipping in—a sort of tidal wave and flood and fire" (quoted in Ludington 1998, 105). Dos Passos joined an ambulance corps in France and experienced his first fighting there. During this time he talked to French soldiers and discovered no hatred of the enemy, only boredom with war (129), and he began to be disillusioned about fighting for a government (136). Eventually he was transferred to the Italian front.

During this time in France and Italy, Dos Passos worked on the manuscript for *One Man's Initiation* (originally published as *First Encounter*). In excerpts from his letters and journals written during the war that he published as part of his introduction to the 1969 edition of the novel, he reveals his attitudes toward the war as he experienced it. These excerpts show a young man enjoying Europe and in particular finding it better than the United States: "[Y]ou hear no jabber about the glory of war: everybody is quite frank about things, amazingly so" (17). Dos Passos's disgust with war propaganda[4] is clear throughout *One Man's Initiation*. The diary simultaneously shows a fascination with war itself: "When one shell comes I want another, nearer, nearer, I constantly feel the need of the drunken excitement of a good bombardment—I want to throw the dice at every turn with the old roisterer, Death" (22). The diaries also show that Dos Passos was reading Rabelais during this time, the effects of which show up in what Cooperman calls the character Martin Howe's view of death as "a gigantic 'circus'" (1967, 95). These feelings lead toward the novel's antihome sentiments, a sense that home is the source of the lies that have trapped these soldiers and that home cannot compete with the seduction of war. The relationship between home and war creates a sense of absurdity that characterizes much of Dos Passos's (and other writers') description of the war; Dos Passos and his companions ate cheese and drank coffee until the military made them go home at 8:30: "Then we wander home and watch the reflections of star-shells on the front beyond the horizon" (1969, 28).

Unlike *Through the Wheat*, which describes a kind of benign distance between home and war, *One Man's Initiation* shows the soldiers' marked hostility toward the American home. At a French theater while on leave, Martin looks directly into the stage lights, reminding him of how "he felt as he had when at home he had leaned over and looked straight into the headlight of an auto drawn up to the side of the road" (94). The conjunction of the drunken revelry at the theater with an image from home suggests the pervading sense of absurdity and unreality that he often experiences in relation to the war. His memory of home shows a sense of unease and entrapment: "'I used to think,' went on Martin, 'that it was my family I must escape from to be free; I mean all the conventional ties, the worship of success and the respectabilities that is drummed into you when you're young.'" Instead, he realizes, the problem is not so much his specific family but American culture in general. Critic Michael Clark argues that the novel explores Howe's discovery that he can't go home: "[T]he novel's purpose is to show that there never was a home, at least not as Howe in his prewar innocence had thought" (1987, 64).

Part of the reason the home never existed, Dos Passos suggests, is because its foundations had been carefully constructed by the media and the government. In America the press misleads people about the war, "gradual lulling to sleep of people's humanity and sense by the phrases, the phrases" (1969, 159). The press and mass media are a source of corruption as well as a medium of corruption used by corrupt men. Linda Wagner, in her study of the structure of *One Man's Initiation*, points out that "Dos Passos sets the unrelieved horror of physical war against the propagandist version of that war, with snatches of popular songs serving as punctuation" (1979, 12). Thus even the rhythm of the text reflects the interweaving of propaganda into the American consciousness.

Howe and other soldiers direct hostility toward the people who believe the war propaganda as well as those who created it. As he travels to France, Martin wonders whether the atrocity stories he has heard are true, only to be told by a girl, "True! Oh, of course it's all true; and lots more that it hasn't been possible to print. . . . If there are any [Germans] left alive after the war they ought to be chloroformed" (Dos Passos 1969, 47–48). Janet Galligani Casey, in *Dos Passos and the Ideology of the Feminine*, points out the connection between women and propaganda in *One Man's Initiation*, calling this girl "an ironic and unselfconscious pin-up girl for a government in need of establishing collective distaste for the enemy" (1998, 73). Significantly, this girl's kind of violent talk coupled with unquestioning belief is feminized, though it is not always women who speak it: "It makes me sick at ma stomach, Howe, to talk to one of those Hun-hatin' women, if they're male or female" (73). For the soldiers, such hatred of the enemy is irrelevant and painful because it shows the noncombatants' ignorance of the soldiers' experiences. Being understood, for the soldiers, is deeply desired but impossible to achieve, made impossible by the very language that has created the war.

Language itself breaks down as soldiers attempt to communicate with noncombatants. One soldier tells of his horror at watching a fellow soldier place a grenade under a wounded German prisoner's pillow; Martin explains to a woman who does not understand the language that "he's telling about a German atrocity," and the woman rotely replies, "Oh, the dirty Germans! What things they've done!" (Dos Passos 1969, 95). The problem, of course, is that it is an Allied soldier who has committed the atrocity, and Martin has to translate this act into something else for the sake of maintaining the home front's perception of the war. To civilians, the words "German atrocity" automatically invoke the propaganda stories of Germans raping women or cutting off boys' hands, while Martin, perhaps intentionally using a misleading term, actually refers to an atrocity committed upon a German prisoner. Martin does not seem to approve of this soldier's act, but by "translating" for the woman, he positions her as outside the community of combatants—outside the group who can truly feel the implications of the story.

The "insiders" are not just Allied soldiers but all soldiers. Martin and his comrades feel closer to Germans than they do to people at home because they have shared similar experiences:

"It's funny," said the little doctor suddenly, "to think how much nearer we are, in state of mind, in everything, to the Germans than to anyone else."

"You mean that the soldiers in the trenches are all further from the people at home than from each other, no matter what side they are on." (71)

Leed comments on the sympathy and identification with the enemy prevalent in the First World War that led to much ritual battle and localized truces (1979, 106–9); this identification "must be regarded as the most important source of the estrangement of those in the trenches from those who demanded offensive activity of the soldier and strove to maintain the aggressive role of the combatant: the staffs and the 'home'" (109). Experiencing the blood, guts, dirt, and boredom of the war has isolated the troops on both sides from the homes they are defending.

"Hun-hatin' women" make the home front undesirable and incomprehensible to Martin. He refuses the cheap sex and hollow love of the prostitutes, dreaming instead of an ideal woman. At one point this woman is the merciful expanse of the sky: "Might not it really be, he kept asking himself, that the sky was a beneficent goddess who would stoop gently out of the infinite spaces and lift him to her breast, where he could lie amid the amber-fringed ruffles of cloud and look curiously down at the spinning ball of the earth?" (Dos Passos 1969, 70) After escaping from prostitutes he thinks of the girl he would like to have with him, "and in her arms he could forget everything but the madness and the mystery and the intricate life of Paris about them" (98). These two incidents suggest that Martin cannot imagine a real romantic relationship. Later he sings about an ideal, hopeless love:

> Where the youth pined away with desire
> And the pale virgin shrouded in snow
> Arise from the graves and aspire
> Where my sunflower wishes to go. (121)

He wants a woman who understands what the war is really like and is capable of helping him forget it or perhaps even understand it, but his song suggests that such a woman not only does not but cannot exist.

Other soldiers also have mixed reactions to the women around them. Martin's friend Tom has found a girl, probably a prostitute, that he would marry; another soldier expresses shock at the "crazy Jane" who lay down with him when he was napping and was "ready for business" when he woke up (73). Perhaps more important, the war has altered the soldiers' relationships to their homes and families. Martin meets a vineyard owner who feels he has lost his connection to his home: "They learn to get on without you" (133). For this man the war is his only life, as he cannot imagine returning to quiet domesticity with his wife, who has also been changed by the war. Yet another soldier is horrified to find a picture of a family on the body of the German soldier he has just bayoneted; he thinks of his own family and wishes he had let the other soldier kill him instead. Had he died, he would have been a hero at home; since he has survived (at least thus far) he has to live with the knowledge that he has killed someone else's husband and father: "Oh, it's shameful! I am ashamed of being a man" (140). This soldier must face the collision of two identities: his public role as a soldier that demands such violence and his private role as a member of a civilized society. Fulfilling the first role precludes his ability to fulfill the second; he does not know how to be a soldier and a father.

Like Claude Wheeler, soldiers in *One Man's Initiation* create their own domestic spaces in the military world and derive a kind of emotional satisfaction from them. Martin and Tom sleep in several different barns; at other times they spend nights in dugouts near the front. In the abri, soldiers sleep while a lieutenant works. For Martin these male spaces provide a kind of comfort, even while the men are exposed to attack:

> Martin sat on the steps of the dugout, looking up the shattered shaft of a tree, from the top of which a few ribbons of bark fluttered against the mauve evening sky. In the quiet he could hear the voices of men chatting in the dark below him, and a sound of someone whistling as he worked. Now and then, like some ungainly bird, a high calibre shell trundled through the air overhead; after its noise had completely died away would come the thud of the explosion. It was like battledore and shuttlecock, these huge masses whirling through the evening far above his head, now from one side, now from the other. It gave him somehow a cosy feeling of safety, as if he were under some sort of bridge over which freight-cars were shunted madly to and fro. (68–69)

Martin's "cosy feeling of safety" in a space under the deadly bombs seems an abnormal reaction, yet in fact in the world of war he has come to expect absurdity and thus finds comfort in its presence. Martin finds an old abbey and dreams of what it would be like to be a monk, secluded with books, away from women. When he comments that he would like to join a monastery, Tom replies, "I'll end up in one, most like, if they don't put me in jail first" (82). The soldiers have become comfortable in their all-male world.

In this world the men have developed their own rituals. Card playing and drinking seem to be the primary activities; Martin sees card playing as imbued with ritual significance: "Is it death they are playing, that they are so merry when they take a trick?" (86) He refuses to participate himself, however, for fear that he will be killed while playing games. Later he observes another ritual: two officers having breakfast; "In their manner there is something that makes Martin see vividly two gentlemen in frockcoats dining at a table under the awning of a café on the boulevards. It has a leisurely ceremoniousness, an ease that could exist nowhere else" (136). The two officers rather formally discuss the religious tendency in human beings even while shells explode around them; they casually pick gravel off their plates and catch falling bottles.[5] The bizarre characteristics of this meal demonstrate that, even in war, men have found ways to ritualize and thus to order their lives.

As in *One of Ours*, here too soldiers take on traditionally female roles. *One Man's Initiation* shows in particular men caring for and nursing other men. Doctors are frequent authority figures, one of whom calls the soldiers "children" (117) and later, in a voice "strident like an angry woman's," drives incoming soldiers out of the abri in order not to crowd the wounded (119). As an ambulance driver, Martin sees the "blood and filth" of the injured soldiers (125). At one point he kneels with a man in the ambulance, "with his chest pressed on the man's chest and one arm stretched down to keep the limp bandaged leg still" (124). Martin's work is rewarded only by an orderly's comment that the patient will soon be dead. Yet Martin finds satisfaction in using his body to help other soldiers, even a German prisoner:

> [H]e felt the arm-muscles and the ribs pressed against his body as he clutched the wounded man tightly to him in the effort of carrying him towards the dugout. The effort gave Martin a strange contentment. It was as if his body were taking part in the agony of this man's body. At last they were washed out, all the hatreds, all the lies, in blood and sweat. Nothing was left but the quiet friendliness of beings alike in every part, eternally alike. (148)

Martin's comfort stems from the fact that they are both men, "beings alike in every part," and because of this likeness they can have between them a "quiet friendliness" even after this extremely physical encounter, suggesting Martin's discomfort with heterosexual relations as constructed by the war ideology. Unlike Claude, who desires genderlessness, Martin specifically desires maleness.

The novel indicates that such a wish cannot be granted beyond the limits of individual bodies. The gendering of noncombatants as feminine

seems to suggest that soldiers, with the experience of war, are their masculine counterpart. Yet the soldiers' feelings of disempowerment seem to
place them also in a feminized position. There are two gendered systems
at work here: soldiers' masculinity in relation to civilians' femininity and
the soldiers' femininity in relation to the masculine, bureaucratic military—and behind the military, the government. The socialist movement
among the French soldiers that Martin joins signals the beginning of a
resistance to a government that strips individuals of selfhood and agency.
But this movement is blown up by the very war fought by the capitalist
government—suggesting that the whole world has become feminized in
relation to an abstract, self-serving government.

Three Soldiers:
The Disintegration of Domesticity and its Implications

While he was in Italy, Dos Passos got in trouble for writing letters protesting the war. His attitude toward the war, Ludington writes, was that "war,
no matter where, consisted of boredom, slavery to all sorts of military stu-
pidities, an interesting sort of misery, and the need for warmth, bread, and
cleanliness. . . . It was no more than an enormous, tragic digression in people's lives which brought death to the intellect, to art, to everything that
mattered" (1998, 158). Dos Passos was eventually sent home, where he
managed to reenlist with an American ambulance unit. During his training at Camp Crane, he spent, for the first time in his life, a significant
amount of time with uneducated, working-class men. He drew on the
people he met there for characters in *Three Soldiers*, which was intended
to be a realistic picture of the war. The characters Chrisfield and Fuselli,
for example, correspond to men Dos Passos met at the camp, and the
novel's emphasis on drinking and whoring comes as well from the attitudes
of the men at Camp Crane (ibid., 170–71).

Looking at elements of domesticity in *Three Soldiers* is particularly
revealing about the way such details, though subsumed in the narrative,
still add meaning to the text. Dos Passos was aware of the importance of
domestic ritual for the maintenance of morale, as shown by his interest in
the scene between the French officers in *One Man's Initiation*. In 1917 he
wrote to his friend Arthur McComb, "Military discipline plus greasy soup
remove all joy of life" (quoted in Ludington 1998, 128). Soldiers' inability to enjoy their bodily existence helps erode individual resistance to
military discipline. In *Three Soldiers* Dos Passos's attention to food reflects
and combines with the power of the military machine to show the suppression of the individual in mechanized war and, more broadly, within a
capitalist society.

In *Three Soldiers* Dos Passos repeatedly describes scenes of men lining up to receive plates of greasy, smelly food and then lining up again to toss their garbage and wash their mess kits in equally greasy water. The novel in fact opens with the pervasiveness of unappetizing food: "The company stood at attention, each man looking straight before him at the empty parade ground, where the cinder piles showed purple with evening. On the wind that smelt of barracks and disinfectant there was a faint greasiness of food cooking" (1997, 7). Eating, rather than being a dignified ritual as experienced by the officers in *One Man's Initiation*, has become an industrial process; the mess hall "had a faint smell of garbage mingled with the smell of the disinfectant the tables had been washed off with after the last meal" (7). Meals are marked by signs that they will soon be over—the smell of garbage—but will inevitably occur again—the smell of disinfectant.

Scenes of eating in the mess hall continue to appear throughout the novel, all of them remarkably similar:

> The oatmeal flopped heavily into the mess-kit. . . . [Fuselli] sat at the dark greasy bench and took a gulp of the scalding coffee that smelt vaguely of dish rags. That woke him up a little. There was little talk in the mess shack. The men, that the bugle had wrenched out of their blankets but fifteen minutes before, sat in rows, eating sullenly or blinking at each other through the misty darkness. (70)

Paired with eating are scenes of washing:

> They were washing their mess-kits in the tub of warm water thick with grease from the hundred mess-kits that had gone before, in front of the shack. An electric light illuminated faintly the wet trunk of a plane tree and the surface of the water where bits of oatmeal floated and coffee grounds,—and the garbage pails with their painted signs: WET GARBAGE, DRY GARBAGE; and the line of men who stood waiting to reach the tub. (70)

The men have become parts of a machine, as critics[6] point out, but it is important to note that it is an organic machine, ingesting food that is the equivalent of garbage in preparation for slaughter on the battlefield, when the soldiers themselves become garbage. One is what one eats, but Dos Passos implies that one is created also by *how* one eats. Whereas the officers in *One Man's Initiation* maintain dignity and a sense of civilization through their ritualized meals, men in *Three Soldiers* have their humanity stripped away simply by the erosion of a respect for their eating.

For Fuselli, such treatment brings about swings in attitude toward the military. On the one hand he misses his aunt's good cooking; on the other hand he wraps himself in his blankets and sleeps as if he were at home. Unlike other characters, he often thinks of his girl at home, hoping to perform actions that will impress her and even writing her in overeager anticipation of his promotion. He is ambitious for his military career but also for his private life: "His head was full of gold and green mouldings and silk and crimson velvet and intricate designs in which naked pink-fleshed cupids writhed indecently. Some day, he was saying to himself, he'd make a hell of a lot of money and live in a house like that with Mabe; no, with Yvonne, or with some other girl" (81). Cooperman argues that Fuselli's honest belief in a system of work and reward fails him; his misreading of Yvonne and his expectation of a romantic relationship with her mark his downfall (1967, 154–55). Fuselli's eventual disgrace lands him, as Cooperman points out, in "a life bound quite literally by horizons of garbage" (152); Iain Colley similarly suggests that the army has wasted the abilities of both Fuselli and Chrisfield (1987, 44). The military machine that feeds Fuselli garbage succeeds in leaving him as garbage in the garbage dump.

The characters' frustrated relationships with women suggests a further separation from satisfying domesticity. Women, like Mabe, Yvonne, and even Genevieve, betray men for reasons that reveal much about their own relationship to the war. Mabe marries a man who didn't go to war; Yvonne replaces Fuselli with a higher-ranked officer; and Genevieve rejects Andrews because of her own idealistic belief in the crusade of the war. Fuselli's, Chrisfield's, and Andrews's relationships with women never achieve intimacy, and, as Casey argues, "the tendency [of the soldiers] to objectify women as symbols or projections of their own needs and desires contributes significantly to their collective characterization as men caught within a system that is impenetrable, larger than the individuals who constitute it, and so insidious and self-perpetuating that its intents, effects, and agents cannot be separated or even discerned" (1998, 85). That is, it is precisely the soldiers' inability to see the women as individuals with any depth that reveals their own implication in the machine of war and the impossibility of their ever truly escaping.

As the novel shifts from Fuselli's story and moves toward a focus on Andrews, the text increasingly omits domestic details. Andrews and Chrisfield enter a village where they observe domesticity, but it is pointedly off limits to them: "Through open doors they could see into comfortable kitchens where copper pots gleamed and where the floors were of clean red tiles" (Dos Passos 1997, 113). They can see the comforts of such a life, but they are not in a position to enjoy it. Later Andrews is invited into the Y man's private rooms, "where a bright fire burned brilliantly in the hearth, lighting up with tongues of red and yellow a square black walnut table and two heavy armchairs with leather backs and bottoms that shone like lacquer" (208). The Y man calls Andrews in for companionship, but for Andrews visits to this room are for business reasons, not personal ones. He does not want a friend but rather someone who can pull strings to get him into the military university program. Andrews next visits the military offices, which in fact are located in "a cube-shaped house" (210); in the military, the public and the private have switched in a disconcerting and bewildering manner. Andrews resents the way the military has taken control of his private life:

> No, he had spent a lifetime in this village being dragged out of his warm blankets every morning by the bugle, shivering as he stood in line for roll call, shuffling in a line that moved slowly past the cookshack, shuffling along in another line to throw what was left of his food into garbage cans, to wash his mess kit in the greasy water a hundred other men had washed their mess kits in; lining up to drill . . . ; lining up twice more for mess, and at last being forced by another bugle into his blankets again to sleep heavily while a smell hung in his nostrils of sweating woolen clothing and breathed-out air and dusty blankets. (213)

After Andrews escapes the military and sheds his uniform, evidence of domestic ritual disappears. He sleeps in rented rooms and eats and drinks what he can afford in cafes. He cannot return to a domestic life or even the imitation one of the military.

For unlike Fuselli, who seems to have accepted his lot in the military life, Andrews's ultimate defiance of the military comes by maintaining the privacy of his spirit. The military has condensed and taken over traditional domestic, private space; even Andrews's room is finally invaded by the MPs. But since Andrews has seen his privacy invaded by the military's control of his eating, sleeping, and clothing, he finds that freedom of mind and spirit is his only resistance: "It's a purely personal matter. I've got to a point where I don't give a damn what happens to me. I don't care if I'm shot, or if I live to be eighty. . . . I'm sick of being ordered round. One more order shouted at my head is not worth living to be eighty" (330).

Jeffrey Walsh argues that for Andrews, war is not a digression from civilization but "the fullest expression of civilization, its fullest metaphor" (1982, 70). It is appropriate, then, that Andrews's life becomes devoid of domesticity, a sign of civilization. Civilization and war become equivalent in *Three Soldiers*, and Andrews finds both to be invasive and oppressive.

Three Soldiers is in some ways one of the most revealing novels about the relationship between war and home: They are both founded on violence and they can both become subject to larger political agendas.

Conclusion

Literature resulting from World War I is, as critics often note, marked by a sense of alienation and betrayal, but reading the meaning of domestic details in such novels provides a greater understanding of why and how soldiers came to feel isolated. Systems of gender roles, reinforced and reinscribed by the necessity of preparing a nation for war, incur resentment against women and against a culture associated with women, even as soldiers find it necessary to reproduce domestic structures in the military world. Yet we see, by the existence of writers such as Cather who write about the battle front and through characters such as Mrs. Wheeler and *Through the Wheat*'s Mrs. Hicks who show that home-front women *can* understand and experience the disillusionment of war and that this resentment against women is misdirected. Further, by examining the inclusion of domestic rituals in these war texts, we see how soldiers attempt to create a sense of control and a sense of self in resistance to the homogenizing force of the military.

Dos Passos once wrote to his friend McComb, "[W]ar is a human phenomenon which you can't argue out of existence" (quoted in Ludington 1998, 92). Scarry argues similarly that no other contest can take the place of war; war both destroys civilization and simultaneously creates it. Claude Wheeler's vision of soldiers as birthing a new world is in some ways borne out by other works about the First World War, yet the disillusionment at the end of *One of Ours* suggests that part of the horror of war is that civilization does not change that much after it, at least not in daily activities. As Armstrong and Tennenhouse argue, violence is fundamental to Western civilization; self-definition requires violence against the Other. A close examination of domestic ritual in war texts shows how our vision has been trained to overlook the presence of domestic detail and the fundamental violence of representation.

Chapter 4
"*Because* Women Have Babies": Hemingway's Soldiers and Their Pregnant Women

Unlike the war novels of Dos Passos, Cather, and Boyd, Ernest Hemingway's World War I writing includes the presence of developed and influential women characters. Both *In Our Time* (1925) and *A Farewell to Arms* (1929) have soldiers as protagonists, yet the relationships of these soldiers with women are a primary impetus for narrative action and interpretation. Dos Passos, Cather, and Boyd generally portray women as absent and often resented; Hemingway, however, depicts women as a much more complicated factor in understanding the emotional and cultural significance of war. In this way Hemingway's writing seems to respond differently to the earlier war novels by women, novels that establish an interdependent ideology between men and women in relation to war. Hemingway's soldiers often resent women, as do Martin Howe, John Andrews, and even Claude Wheeler, yet they are also drawn to women, not merely as prostitutes but also as caregivers, lovers, friends, and homemakers.

Many critics have focused on Hemingway's relationship to gender. Judith Fetterley, for example, attacks Hemingway as a misogynist who sees women only as mirrors for men's self-image (1977). Mark Spilka, in *Hemingway's Quarrel with Androgyny*, discusses Hemingway's exploration of both masculine and feminine roles, concluding that Hemingway's works portray a fear of the feminine and an emphasis on masculinity (1990). In "Hemingway's Gender Training" Jamie Barlowe contextualizes Hemingway's experience with gender beyond that of his family circle; that is, she explains the social and political activities of the women's movement before and during Hemingway's lifetime (2000). This social question of gender focused primarily on definitions of femininity, Barlowe points out, while "[t]he social constructions of white, middle-class manhood . . . was not under much contestation or public debate, especially when a series of wars reinforced masculinized notions of duty, honor, and courage" (128). She claims that accordingly Hemingway's men are more interesting than his women because he had a more difficult time defining masculinity (130). Hemingway's approach to gender is as complicated and contradictory as is that of his critics.

I believe that Hemingway recognized the complexity of both masculinity and femininity as well as the dependent relationship between those concepts and that his war writings provide an opportunity to explore what happens to masculinity when femininity changes. In regard to Hemingway's war writing, the connection between gender and violence is particularly relevant, and I find Nancy Huston's "Matrix of War" to be a useful framework for exploring this connection (1986). Huston discusses the relationship in myths between men, women, and war, specifically the paired, gendered activities of childbirth and fighting. She explains that "the symbolic equivalence between childbirth and war might be said to be one of the rare constants of human culture" even while she maintains that "they have traditionally been perceived as mutually exclusive" (127). That is, although women, mothers in particular, are excluded from the realms of hunting and combat, the glory men achieve on the battlefield is described in similar terms as the pain women experience in childbirth. Huston uses the term "reciprocal metaphorization" to describe the back-and-forth linkage between fighting and childbearing (131). Even though she argues that it is women's ability to have children that inspires men to fight, I think the term reciprocal metaphorization usefully implies a lack of cause and effect—that is, the term conveys a sense of mutual origination. Ideas about war and childbirth circle each other, taking on different meanings as one or the other takes on different symbolic meanings.

In Our Time and A Farewell to Arms show both a fear of the domestic world and a longing for the security domestic ritual can bring. Hemingway's texts show a reliance on domestic details and rituals to a greater extent than the war novels of Dos Passos and Boyd. Hemingway not only perhaps saw the origins of war in domestic ideology, as Dos Passos and Boyd did, but also attempted to show the changes such a highly gendered environment as war would make in domesticity. The rituals of male activities such as war, drinking, sports, and bullfighting are prominent Hemingway themes, yet few critics note that Hemingway also concerns himself with ritual of a "feminine" kind. His war novels show characters, male and female, shaping, relying on, and enjoying domestic life—perhaps because of the ritualized aspects of such a life. Whether it is the ritual of a bullfight or the ritual of making coffee, Hemingway sees in such ordered activities a human need to make sense of the world and to find in it a sense of security and identity. Ritual is and bestows power.

In Our Time: From Home to War and Back Again

Hemingway's *In Our Time* foregrounds male experience before, during, and after World War I, but domesticity, imaged in part by pregnant women, forms the necessary context for this experience. Understanding his technique of juxtaposition helps bring together the diverse elements in the collection, making meaning of the seemingly disparate events. Critics have suggested various strategies for understanding the relationship of the stories to the interchapters; Jackson J. Benson, for example, points out repeated images of violence, screams, sex, birth, and death in the collection (1983). Similarly, Richard Hasbany argues that *In Our Time* is united by the techniques of imagism: a focus on words and images that leads to an interplay between those images (1974). I believe that awareness of the domestic images—those of eating, cooking, childbirth, and relationships—can lead to an understanding of both the disruptions and continuities that thread the pieces of *In Our Time*. For example, in the opening story, "On the Quai at Smyrna," the narrator comments on the women giving birth, in particular on the women whose babies died: "You couldn't get the women to give up their dead babies. They'd have babies dead for six days" (Hemingway 1958, 12). The dead babies both reflect the destruction of the present and suggest darkness in the future. Yet while masculine concerns with war and military occupation fill the consciousness of the narrator, the women are moving forward with life apart from the war. Wayne B. Stengel points out that "ultimately, it is [the narrator's] isolated vision of childbirth that undermines the complete devastation of this refugee encampment and yet makes it doubly grisly. Something still lives or struggles to live amidst this masculine vision of destruction. Throughout *In Our Time*, one male voice attempts to cover, evade, or efface these views of female fecundity" (1994, 90). "On the Quai at Smyrna" establishes a context through which men view pregnant women throughout the rest of the collection, as these women signify men's loss of control amidst chaos and violence.

In Our Time only marginally touches on the actual fighting of the First World War; in fact the war is much less present than the domestic world. The text offers glimpses of war in the early interchapters, and at the same time some of these interchapters describe domesticity and its disruptions at the front. For example, in chapter 1 the kitchen corporal describes how "the adjutant kept riding up alongside my kitchen and saying, 'You must put it out. It is dangerous. It will be observed.' We were fifty kilometers from the front but the adjutant worried about the fire in my kitchen" (Hemingway 1958, 13). Here, domestic tools have become a source of danger for soldiers—just as they have in *One of Ours*, when a lit match becomes a military target and stew almost scalds a captain. In the same chapter, "women and kids were in the carts crouched with mattresses, mirrors, sewing machines, bundles. There was a woman having a kid with a young girl holding a blanket over her and crying" (21). The evacuation has displaced the home and domestic activities, and by Chapter VI, when Nick is wounded, the home is physically destroyed: "The pink wall of the house opposite had fallen out from the roof, and an iron bedstead hung twisted toward the street. Two Austrian dead lay in the rubble in the shade of the house" (63). In Chapter VII Nick mocks domesticity by going upstairs with a prostitute. After Chapter IX the war and the domestic disappear from the interchapters entirely, replaced by the bullfighting vignettes. But the early interchapters remain images that are juxtaposed with and against the stories and must be kept in mind in order to understand the stories.

The stories of In Our Time show domestic life, in its existing form, usually to be entrapping and stifling for men. In "The Doctor and the Doctor's Wife," the wife is a passive-aggressive woman who controls her entire house with her sighs of pain and her penetrating voice that traps the doctor in conversations he does not wish to have. He and his son feel the need to escape his wife's control by retreating outdoors. In "The End of Something," Marjorie represents domesticity by bringing the blanket and the picnic food; later, in "The Three-Day Blow," Bill tells Nick how lucky he is to escape marriage with Marjorie: "Once a man's married he's absolutely bitched. . . . He hasn't got anything more. Nothing. Not a damn thing. He's done for" (47). He claims Nick would have to marry Marjorie's whole family: "Imagine having them around the house all the time and going to Sunday dinners at their house, and having them over to dinner and [Marjorie's mother] telling Marge all the time what to do and how to act" (47). Bill imagines domestic life to be entrapping, for both Nick and Marjorie.

But despite Nick's experience of his parents' unhappy marriage, Bill's image of Marjorie and domestic life is not necessarily Nick's. In "'Nothing Was Ever Lost': Another Look at 'That Marge Business,'" H. R. Stoneback argues that Marjorie displays great dignity in response to Nick's rejection and that Nick feels her loss profoundly (1995). Linda Wagner comments that Marjorie has already achieved the "semi-stoic self awareness which Hemingway's men have, usually, yet to attain" (1981, 63). Indeed Marjorie is competent in outdoor activities, not merely domestic ones; she rows the boat, sets up fishing lines, and cleans fish. And despite Nick's claim that "I've taught you everything," he now feels that "you know everything. That's the trouble" (Hemingway 1958, 34). He has nothing further to teach her and thus the relationship is no longer "fun." Although at first he may have been drawn to Marjorie's difference from his mother, he comes to feel that her competence in both indoor and outdoor matters leaves him with no role, and thus, like his father, he is powerless in the relationship. At the end of "The Three-Day Blow" Nick is comforted by the thought that he and Marjorie might get back together; subsequent stories, however, reveal that this does not happen. The brush with domesticity proves to be both comforting and frustrating for Nick.

In Our Time shows that after the war, the home becomes even more a structure of confinement and disorientation. As Stengel argues, "'Soldier's Home' . . . is one of the central stories in American literature about shell-shocked return to false domestic tranquillity by an aesthetic sensibility that has deeply confused the rites of war and American gamesmanship with how to avoid feminine control" (1994, 93). Krebs feels stifled in his home and his hometown and must eventually leave both. He feels incapable of negotiating the new dating rituals as well as of fulfilling his parents' expectations. Other stories show that for soldiers who lost their sense of autonomy during the war, pregnant women add to and complicate an already-present fear of powerlessness. As a soldier in the First World War, Nick discovers his lack of control over the future; the violence of war defies logic. And for Nick, whose first experience with childbirth in "Indian Camp" involves the death of the father, Helen's pregnancy must also signify a threat to himself. Further, the figure of the pregnant woman invokes fear of the loss of (male) independence, especially through memories of the controlling mother; the domineering and manipulative Mrs. Adams is the figure against which both Nick and his father assert their independence in "The Doctor and the Doctor's Wife." The narrative style of *In Our Time* forces the reader to place Helen's pregnancy against the background of the first story; images of pregnant women on the pier in "On the Quai at Smyrna," juxtaposed with Nick's memories of childhood, suggest that pregnancy involves violence—for the father and for the soldier.

How the father/soldier handles such insecurity and threat of violence is integral to the stories of *In Our Time*; the pregnant woman requires her husband to reconcile anxiety about the future with a loss of control. On the illegal fishing trip in "Out of Season" the young, possibly pregnant, wife[1] taunts her husband, "Of course you haven't got the guts to just go back" (Hemingway 1958, 100). She herself leaves and in so doing forces her husband to consider the consequences of his actions. She demands that he reevaluate his definition of manhood since what is masculine in a single, childless man is no longer masculine in a man with children to provide for. As a prospective father, he cannot risk breaking the law and spending time in jail. For Nick, too, pregnancy requires that he face a loss of personal autonomy. George asks, "It's hell, isn't it?" (111), referring to the upcoming changes in Nick's life. Nick, however, answers, "No. Not exactly" (111). Although his later remarks convey his expectation of reduced independence, he seems to have found some compensations in Helen's pregnancy, such as the satisfaction of love and family. Perhaps these compensations also take the form of Nick's relief at not having been rendered impotent during the war (luckily avoiding the fate of Jake Barnes). In this case pregnancy has the power to affirm manhood. As David J. Ferrero argues, Nick does not rebel against Helen and the baby but accepts his upcoming fatherhood with an understandable sadness at the loss of his more carefree youth (1998, 26). Significantly, Helen also apparently has mixed feelings about the pregnancy and the changes the baby will cause, suggesting that anxiety about the future produced by pregnancy is not limited to men.

If homes with women are fraught with apprehension, homes without them seem, on the surface, to be an attractive alternative. In "The Three-Day Blow," Nick and Bill fall into a domestic routine in which Nick warms his feet while Bill brings him dry socks. The house, occupied by only Bill and his father, is a retreat for Nick, who sometimes sleeps there too. In "The Battler," Nick stumbles into an outdoor domestic setting, where the former fighter and his friend have set up camp. The dinner Bugs cooks is described in detail: "Into the skillet he was laying slices of ham. As the skillet grew hot the grease sputtered and Bugs . . . turned the ham and broke eggs into the skillet, tipping it from side to side to baste the eggs with the hot fat" (Hemingway 1958, 57). After Ad Francis tries to attack Nick, Bugs asks Nick to leave, in the politest terms: "I wish we could ask you to stay the night but it's just out of the question. Would you like to take some of that ham and some bread with you?" (62). The homeless men have their own system of domesticity and hospitality. In "Cross-Country Snow," George daydreams about getting away from a settled life:

> Gee, Mike, don't you wish we could just bum together? Take our skis and go on the train to where there was good running and then go on and put up at pubs and go right across the Oberland and up the Valais and all through the Engadine and just take repair kits and extra sweaters and pyjamas in our rucksacks and not give a damn about school or anything. (110)

He wishes to trade home for pubs and replace entrapping domestic accoutrements with "repair kits and extra sweaters and pyjamas." This desire for male mobility, however, does not seem to appeal to Nick. Underneath these scenes of male domesticity lies a sense of impermanence, tension, and unfulfillment.

Instead, "The Big Two-Hearted River" shows Nick's desire for a solitary male home. He sets up his camp with detailed care:

> Already there was something mysterious and homelike. Nick was happy as he crawled inside the tent. He had not been unhappy all day. This was different though. Now things were done. There had been this to do. Now it was done. . . . He had made his camp. He was settled. Nothing could touch him. It was a good place to camp. He was there, in the good place. He was in his home where he had made it. (139)

Nick does not like being unsettled; the need to set up the camp had been hanging over him. Once the camp is made, however, he is safe within his own handiwork, responsible to no one else within his own domestic sphere. The description of his cooking, like that in "The Battler," is detailed and extensive, telling what he cooks and how he cooks it. In his mind he runs over an argument he once had with a friend about the best way to make coffee. The rituals of domesticity have a soothing power, whether the actions are performed by men or by women; in this way *In Our Time* shows the arbitrary nature of the assignment of gender roles and the constriction caused by social enforcement of female-centered domesticity.

Frederic Henry's Domestic World, Catherine Barkley's Battle Experience

Whereas *In Our Time* ends with isolated male domesticity, *A Farewell to Arms* works in the other direction, from male domesticity to restructuring domestic heterosexual relationships in the context of the First World War. In the time between writing the two works, Hemingway left his first wife Hadley and married Pauline Pfeiffer; Pauline's dangerous pregnancy and Caesarian delivery as well as guilt at his abandoning Hadley were prominent issues for Hemingway. *A Farewell to Arms* shows a domesticity beset by outside forces rather than by individual suffocation as in *In Our Time*. The later novel also focuses more on the First World War itself; thus domesticity and domestic ritual at the front stand in comparison to his treatment of domesticity behind the lines of battle.

A Farewell to Arms emphasizes the importance of home places. As Frederic Henry travels from station to station and from the front during the retreat, he often describes houses, and the military and medical personnel are quartered in the houses of evacuated citizens. He enjoys "a house in Gorizia that had a fountain and many thick shady trees in a walled garden and a wisteria vine." He is pleased too that "the Austrians seemed to want to come back to the town some time, if the war should end, because they did not bombard it to destroy it but only a little in a military way" (Hemingway 1957, 5). During his scenic drive to the front, too, Frederic notices damaged homes, the "broken houses of the little town that was to be taken" (45). During the retreat, Frederic pays atten-tion to the farmhouses they pass, and he protects one house from looting by the two sergeants one of the drivers has picked up. As they leave, he looks back: "It was a fine, low, solid stone house and the ironwork of the well was very good" (202). Noticeably, Frederic does not comment on the people who must have lived in these houses or on their fates. It is the shell of the domestic world that he sees, not the soul.

The novel does, however, evoke central issues of domesticity by describing the ritual of eating in great detail. The text often mentions specifically what the characters eat and how they eat it. During dinner at the mess Frederic relates how the men eat by "lifting the spaghetti on the fork until the loose strands hung clear then lowering it into the mouth, or else using a continuous lift and sucking into the mouth, helping ourselves to wine from the grass-covered gallon flask" (7). Just before he is wound-ed, Frederic caters to the demands of his men for food, bringing them macaroni and cheese; as a result of an earlier conversation with his dri-vers about socialism, Frederic here dispenses with military hierarchy: "No. . . . Put it on the floor. We'll all eat" (53). They sit about the pot as a group, "all eating, holding their chins close over the basin, tipping their heads back, sucking in the ends" (54). With these descriptions Frederic reveals his attunement to relationships within the group and how they can be symbolically expressed. Later, during the retreat, the soldiers complain about the lack of food, and Frederic comments: "[Food] can't win a war but it can lose one" (184). He refers both to the practical, physical need for food in order for soldiers to work and fight and also to the psycholog-ical need for food in order for soldiers to feel that their country supports them in their efforts and to bond with their fellow soldiers in the ritual-istic eating of it. The eating of food at the front is a communal act, just as it is in the home. This point is emphasized by the soldiers finding and drinking wine they assume has been saved for a wedding (217). The drinking of the wine shows the easy translation of family ritual into mili-tary ritual. The fact that the wine has gone bad may reflect the darkness behind the ritual of eating and drinking during a time of violence and upheaval.

For the novel shows that eating during war has become a dangerous activity as well as a ritual. Frederic is wounded when the dugout in which he is eating is bombed. Critics have often pointed to the impersonality of death in the First World War; the shells can hit at any time. Stanley Cooperman comments that Frederic is frightened by "the horror of male passivity" (1967, 182), and indeed technological warfare has made the soldiers into helpless targets. Frederic is specifically affected by being wounded during a domestic ritual; when Rinaldi tries to say Frederic is a hero, Frederic denies any heroism with the comment, "I was blown up while we were eating cheese" (Hemingway 1957, 63). Although Rinaldi and others try to make any wounding a cause for heroism precisely because of their "horror of male passivity" in the war, Frederic is not afraid to face facts and even seems to find a kind of satisfaction in the circumstances of his injury. He seems to be comforted by the knowledge that he was not wounded during a foreign activity like killing the enemy but rather during a familiar activity, one he can understand.

Frederic equates war and the reasons for fighting with the protection of the domestic world. With his drivers, who are socialists and resent the war, he argues that fighting is necessary:

> "What is defeat? You go home."
> "They come after you. They take your home. They take your sisters."
> "I don't believe it," Passini said. "They can't do that to everybody. Let everybody defend his home. Let them keep their sisters in the house." (50)

The drivers challenge the propaganda that brings the United States into the war and in which Frederic still needs to believe. He desperately desires a safe place for himself and for the performance of rituals that creates a sense of comfort and familiarity.

Throughout *A Farewell to Arms* Frederic sets up and lives in a number of temporary homes. Critics often discuss the housekeeping he sets up with Catherine Barkley, but before he lives with Catherine he lives with his friend Rinaldi. They share a room in their house behind the lines, a room described in a mixture of domestic and military terms:

> The window was open, my bed was made up with blankets and my things hung on the wall, the gas mask in an oblong tin can, the steel helmet on the same peg. At the foot of the bed was my flat trunk, and my winter boots, the leather shiny with oil, were on the trunk. My Austrian sniper's rifle with its blued octagon barrel and the lovely dark walnut, cheek-fitted, *schutzen* stock, hung over the two beds. (11)

This home shows a fusion of domestic comfort with military necessity. With Rinaldi Frederic shares a home and a close relationship; Rinaldi, referring to his professional ability to doctor soldiers, speaks to Frederic in markedly sexual language: "I would take you and never hurt you" (64). This homoerotic tension between the two men is deferred by their continual references to women, especially prostitutes. Before Frederic leaves on the retreat he spends his last night in the room that he shared with Rinaldi but sleeps in Rinaldi's bed rather than his own. Regardless of whether Rinaldi has sexual feelings for Frederic (and vice versa), Frederic finds with Rinaldi a sense of home and family, with Rinaldi as both brother and mother.

With Catherine, Frederic shows a simultaneous desire for and resistance to setting up a truly domestic existence. On leave before meeting Catherine, Frederic sleeps with a number of women, but those experiences always leave him feeling empty:

> I had gone . . . to the smoke of cafes and nights when the room whirled and you needed to look at the wall to make it stop, nights in bed, drunk, . . . sure that this was all and all and all and not caring. Suddenly to care very much and to sleep to wake with it sometimes morning and all that had been there gone and everything sharp and hard and clear and sometimes a dispute about the cost. (13)

At first he sees Catherine as only a diversion from the prostitutes and has no intention of falling in love with her, but when she arrives at the hospital he finds himself immediately in love. Judith Fetterley sees this reaction as evidence of Frederic's selfish immaturity (1977, 56), yet Frederic's need for Catherine goes beyond a simple need for someone to take care of him and to comfort his "horror of male passivity." Catherine helps Frederic create a home place, as Rinaldi did at the front; Frederic's tendency "suddenly to care very much" when he is with prostitutes suggests a longing for an emotional fulfillment that can be met only by a stable emotional relationship. The suddenness with which Frederic both "cares very much" and falls in love with Catherine makes the depth of the emotion suspect, but it also reveals an already-established need for domesticity. Frederic says repeatedly that he goes "home to the hospital" (Hemingway 1957, 117, 118, 134). But this domestic space has even less legitimacy than his room with Rinaldi, for in the hospital the lovers are together only in secret and would be separated if it were publicly known they were sharing a room.

Part of Frederic and Catherine's strength as a couple is their ability to create a home wherever they are. They have the hospital, various hotel rooms, and even the enclosure of Frederic's cape. After his desertion from the Italian army, Frederic and Catherine create a home in the hotel at Stresa:

That night at the hotel, in our room with the long empty hall outside and our shoes outside the door, a thick carpet on the floor of the room, outside the windows the rain falling and in the room light and pleasant and cheerful, then the light out and it exciting with smooth sheets and the bed comfortable, feeling that we had come home, feeling no longer alone. (249)

When they arrive in Lausanne for the birth of their child, Catherine comments:

"I have to try and make this room look like something."
"Like what?"
"Like our home."
"Hang out the Allied flags." (309)

Frederic jokes that the war has been their home; the source of their domesticity is not a place but an event.

Frederic and Catherine's relationship is a ritual displaced, a marriage made in the new circumstances of war. In pre-war times, a love affair might take a "natural" course to marriage and then to sex and children. During war, however, marriage postpones sex and children, since, as Catherine points out, if they were to get married they would be separated immediately. Catherine's friend Fergy's comment that "you'll fight before you marry" (108) is telling; she may be suggesting that the two lovers are incompatible, but she may also be referring to an interruption of traditional courting and marriage rituals. That is, in the normal course of events couples fight *after* they marry, but by rushing their sexual relationship and disrupting expected patterns Frederic and Catherine may fight *before* they marry, hence permanently breaking off the path to marriage.

Frederic has mixed feelings about actually being married, but he does not seem to realize that Catherine may not be eager to be married either. Catherine is a VAD, meaning, as she says, that she works hard but no one trusts her until there is a crisis (25). In "Corpus/Corps/Corpse: Writing the Body at War," Jane Marcus explains the social ramifications of being a VAD: Well-bred women volunteered to go to the front to do the dirty work of war—dealing with blood, guts, and shit—much to the embarrassment of others, whose sensibilities were offended by middle- and upper-class women doing such work (1989, 124–25). Sandra Whipple Spanier argues that Catherine already knows about the war when she meets Frederic (1990). Her lover has been killed at the Somme so she knows about technological warfare and its impersonality, and as a result Catherine has seen the pointlessness of maintaining the old standards.

She refused to sleep with her first lover because "I didn't know about any-thing then. I thought it would be worse for him. I thought perhaps he couldn't stand it and then of course he was killed and that was the end of it" (Hemingway 1957, 19). She also had the "silly idea" that her fiancé would show up at her hospital with a sabre cut; instead "they blew him all to bits" (20). When Frederic, her replacement lover, shows up at her hos-pital with a blown-apart leg, Catherine cares for him calmly and effi-ciently. She takes responsibility for the pregnancy, mentioning that she has done something to prevent or get rid of it and failed, and telling her friend Fergy that "I get in my own messes" (246). With the new world of war, Catherine realizes, she cannot count on anyone else to keep her out of messes. She knows, as Frederic does not, that men are not fighting for her honor but rather to protect and restore their own manhood. She her-self must take responsibility for protecting her honor, if she wants to pro-tect it, but instead of maintaining her chastity she redefines the notion of "honor," living according to her own loyalties and loves.

Despite Catherine's much-documented selfless love for Frederic and her comfort in domestic spaces, she is not really a domestic woman. On the boat trip to Switzerland, Frederic cautions her not to let the oar hit her in the stomach, but Catherine responds, "If it did . . . life might be much simpler" (275). Like Helen in "Cross-Country Snow," she is not pleased about the implications of having a child for herself and her lifestyle. She worries that "she won't come between us, will she? The lit-tle brat" (304), expressing a fear of family life and of the mothering role that will divert her availability from Frederic. She also shows her igno-rance of what a baby's needs are:

> "There aren't many people reach my time without baby things."
> "You can buy them."
> "I know. That's what I'll do tomorrow. I'll find out what is necessary."
> "You ought to know. You were a nurse."
> "But so few of the soldiers had babies in the hospitals." (308)

Catherine disproves any idea that women automatically know how to mother or even that nursing is directly connected to domesticity.

Frederic and Catherine's relationship shows the weakness of social institutions to provide structure and security during the upheaval of war. During Catherine's labor, Frederic reflects on her suffering for their nights of passion: "This was what people got for loving each other. . . . You never got away with anything. Get away hell! It would have been the same if we had been married fifty times" (320). The ritual of marriage is no pro-tection from the dangers of nature. Society might disapprove of their relationship, but, as Michael Reynolds argues, the ultimate judge is biology and poor doctoring (1996). Domesticity is what the lovers desire, not marriage, for domesticity brings comfort and security whereas marriage, in war, brings separation, anxiety, and greater enforcement of gender roles. Yet domesticity is itself a social institution or at least a response to socially created needs. Catherine's death is thus even more disturbing for Frederic: His emotional need for a heterosexual, domestic partnership, filled during war in an unorthodox relationship, is still subject to being undermined. Domesticity, which offered him comfort when the rest of the world as he knew it fell apart, is also vulnerable—and made vulnerable by the very act that is at its heart. Most of Catherine and Frederic's domestic happiness takes place in hospital and hotel beds, and sex turns out to be traitorous and destructive to their relationship.

The violence that war does to domesticity and social institutions is anticipated by the novel's opening image of soldiers as pregnant women: "[T]he men, passing on the road, marched as though they were six months gone with child" (Hemingway 1957, 4). What causes this visual effect is the accoutrements of military necessity: rifles and ammunition. The soldiers will give birth not to a living being but to violence and death—foreshadowing the bloody and fatal end of Catherine's pregnancy. For both the soldiers and for Catherine "pregnancy" signifies not hope for the future but entrapment and danger. Death for soldiers can come at any time, unsuspected, just as for women, especially before medical advances of the later twentieth century, death can accompany childbirth.[2]

Many critics have speculated on the narrative necessity that Catherine die as well as the implications of her death for Frederic. Cooperman suggests that Catherine's death castrates Frederic (1967, 183); Fetterley claims, "Frederic needs to feel betrayed and Catherine serves this need" (1977, 63). Spanier points out that it is Catherine who acts with a true soldier's ability to live in the moment, Catherine who is the real "Hemingway hero," showing Frederic how to die with little fuss (1990, 80). But Catherine's death also suggests Hemingway's failure to imagine a new role for women, a way to transform the liberated Catherine into a mother. How could she be transformed from a "Hemingway hero" to a wife and mother?

As the system of signification described in Huston's "Matrix of War" shows, the hero and the mother cannot be combined in a single person (1986). The tensions of domesticity laid out in *In Our Time* are explored further in *A Farewell to Arms*, but the latter novel, like the former work, still ends with a solitary male figure. Masculinity changes when femininity does, and correspondingly the nature of domesticity changes. It is this mutable domesticity that Hemingway seems to find so unsettling. The

First World War, it is argued, showed the world the fragility of Western civilization and the instability of its foundations; for Hemingway this exposure of civilization's cracks includes the revelation of an inconstant domesticity, leaving men to find and create home places for themselves. For women, this mutable domesticity ultimately means their erasure from Hemingway's world; as Catherine Barkley shows, the collision of the stoic hero with the mother figure creates, simply, absence—a literary black hole.

Conclusion

By bringing together soldiers with women, especially pregnant women and the domesticity they signify, Hemingway recognizes the inseparability of battle front and home front. The desire for "home" is, he shows, unrelated to gender, although expectations about who maintains that home remain constant in a heterosexual society. When women, paired with soldiers, become pregnant, they become visible representatives of daily life and of a gendered domestic system that competes with the supposedly ungendered world of the military. These women throw into relief the unquestioned assumptions about domesticity and challenge the pairing of women with home; both Helen's and Catherine's reluctance to accept motherhood suggests that the war has shown them too that previously unchallenged views about women are limiting and, for Catherine, dangerous.

A Farewell to Arms retrospectively anticipates the postwar world of In Our Time, when the fighting ends and with it the all-male military sphere. Frederic Henry leaves the war with no wife and no child, but Nick Adams does marry; in both cases the soldier must come out of the liminal space of war—a space where expectations are to some degree lifted, where Frederic and Catherine can be more married by not getting married—and return to a society that has not experienced such liminality. The end of the war signifies a return to domesticity and inscribed expectations about heterosexual relationships.

Chapter 5
The Return of the Dead to the American Family

Frederic Henry, leaving the body of Catherine Barkley, walks through the rain and returns to his hotel. Although many Hemingway soldiers (Nick Adams, Jake Barnes) remain in Europe at least for awhile after the war, most U.S. soldiers, like Hemingway's Harold Krebs, returned to the United States. For many young American men, the First World War was a broadening experience, in both negative and positive ways; they saw the violence of war, and they saw exotic Europe.[1] But after the war, American soldiers returned to a way of life that for many of them no longer seemed to fit. When they came back to the States, soldiers had to face changes in themselves as well as in American society—its differences and its now-unfamiliar similarities to the world they had left. Their families and communities, in turn, had to come to terms with changes in their men.

When the U.S. soldier left for war, he committed himself to a specific ideological system that defined his identity, his nation, and his place in society. Eric Leed, speaking of European soldiers as well as American, describes this commitment as an "economy of sacrifice" in which "the civilian exchanged his private self and his individual self-interest for a public and communal identity represented in the uniform. For this temporary loss of a private self, the soldier can demand restitution in the form of honor, prestige, or financial rewards" (1979, 204). The U.S. soldier was additionally invested in a gender system that defined his relationship to war and to his home. The ideological system put forth by propaganda and sentimental literature created an interdependency between the soldier and the "Beautiful Soul," a matrix within which men fought for the women—wives and mothers—they loved, just as women loved their men so they could fight.

During his participation in the war, however, the soldier discovered that despite his sacrifice of his individual identity for his nation, the nation got along without him. He saw in capitalist nations such as the United States, for example, that some people actually profited financially through the sacrifice of his blood, dignity, and friends. Thus the soldier perceived that his contract with his nation and community was "disrupted"; "this disrup-tion was experienced as the fragmentation of the moral nexus between front and home, the nexus that made the suffering and death at the front meaningful in terms of the preservation of the larger entity, the 'nation,' the home" (Leed 1979, 204). The soldier experienced anger at a society that sent him to war with a hollow ideology and that profited through vio-lation of that ideology. Soldiers such as Dos Passos's Dan Fuselli lose their girl at home; others, such as Martin Howe, reject the ideology of home; still others, such as William Hicks, learn shocking things about their families, such as his mother's willingness to send him cyanide.

The disillusioned, ungrounded soldier is the most common image of the World War I veteran in American literature. As Frederick Hoffman writes, "[t]he war had itself been so violent a departure from custom, from 'the rules,' that it was almost impossible to return to them. One either went away or tried to change the rules" (1955, 76). Writers addressed soldiers' response both to these "rules" of American society and to the changing quicksand of the rules themselves. Hemingway's story "Soldier's Home" (1925) is one example of the issues that a veteran of the First World War faced when he returned home. Harold Krebs finds that no one understands him— people expect him to lie about his experiences—and this lack of understanding takes away his sense of peace with himself: "[T]he times so long back when he had done the one thing, the only thing for a man to do, easily and naturally, when he might have done something else, now lost their cool, valuable quality and then were lost themselves" (1958, 69–70). The skills that he acquired are no longer useful, and the community's refusal or inability to affirm his experi-ences makes him lose the sense of himself that he had been able to construct during the war. He had been a "good soldier" (72), but at home he drifts: sleeping late, reading, becoming bored, playing pool.

Krebs's psychological malaise is a typical reaction of the World War I veteran. Leed suggests that the returning soldier experienced a profound, deeply internalized disruption of self caused by the disjunction between home and war. At the front, soldiers' sense of themselves was destroyed by mechanized warfare; their hope for a preserved, whole identity was tied to the home:

> The idealization of the "men and things of the past," those scenes and peo-ple that came to seem ever more distant in the trenches, preserved some sense of a possible continuity and sameness, some hope for a unified iden-tity. These idealizations often shattered under the impact of demobiliza-tion, unemployment, poverty, and the sheer strangeness of what was once familiar. (1979, 189)

The reality of home could not withstand the ideological pressure the soldiers' experience of war placed on it. Leed points out that "shell shock," or cases of psychological trauma related to the war, actually increased after the war was over and that in the United States—more than twenty years after World War I—58 percent of the patients cared for in veterans' hospitals were psychiatric cases (185). Leed concludes that "the most lasting pathologies of war represented the consequences that result when the individual loses his sense of himself as an autonomous actor in a manipulable world" (186). The harm done to the self by industrial warfare was permanent and perhaps made worse by the soldiers' return to the domestic world; when Cather's Mrs. Wheeler is quietly glad that her son Claude does not return to American society, her insight into the psyche of a soldier is profound.

Yet many soldiers returned to the United States and were able, more or less successfully, to reincorporate themselves into American society. Even "Soldier's Home" suggests that Harold will find a job—not in his town, perhaps, but in the larger Kansas City—and somehow make his way: "He would go to Kansas City and get a job and [his mother] would feel all right about it. There would be one more scene maybe before he got away. He would not go down to his father's office. He would miss that one. He wanted his life to go smoothly. It had just gotten going that way" (1958, 77).

Understanding soldiers' process of adjustment to life back home requires an examination of the reception they received and the changes in American society that occurred during and after the war. Noncombatants met the returning veterans with a variety of complicated attitudes, ranging from misguided benevolence to distrust and hostility. David Kennedy points out that most U.S. civilians had only a vague idea of what the soldiers had experienced in Europe (1980, 228). The soldiers went abroad with visions of glory and self-sacrifice and a belief in an ideology of war that was blown, quite literally, away; men and women at home, who did not experience the shock of industrial warfare, continued to maintain their beliefs. People in Krebs's town "had heard too many atrocity stories to be thrilled by actualities" (1958, 69). Mrs. Krebs, in comparing her son's experiences to those of her father in the Civil War, is typical in her misunderstanding of the First World War. Returning veterans were treated as heroes by some, but they were also perceived as a threat: men "who had to be reintegrated, reacculturated, reeducated" (Leed 1979, 196). Krebs's father's discomfort with his son exemplifies this fear of the soldier: the civilian's need for the veteran to find a job and a wife and settle down to a "normal" American life.

The social structure and attitudes of the United States changed during the war years. Although many disenfranchised groups, such as women and African Americans, had hoped that the war might bring them social advances, actual reforms were few. As David Kennedy argues, "[t]he war had not massively dislocated American material life, creating pressure for further change, and though it had violently agitated the nation's spirit, it had not touched it deeply. The conflict was too remote, and American participation too short, to have worked transformations in 'thought and ideals' " (1980, 247). Women got the vote in 1920, but visions of women flooding the workforce were not based in fact; Kennedy shows that fewer women were employed outside the home in 1920 than were in 1910 (285).[2] Using the concept of "the double helix," Margaret R. Higonnet and Patrice L.-R. Higonnet demonstrate that getting the vote and even jobs did not ensure freedom or security for women (1987, 6–7); that is, with the return of the men, women, and their work were devalued in order to prevent "feminizing" the soldiers. Joan Scott argues that "war is represented as a sexual disorder; peace thus implies a return to 'traditional' gender relationships, the familiar and natural order of families, men in public roles, women at home, and so on" (1987, 27). The postwar climate pressured citizens to return to more restrictive ideas about gender, class, and race.

"Soldier's Home" explores Krebs's introduction to a new world of gender relations. He discovers in his home town that "[n]othing was changed . . . except that the young girls had grown up." And they have grown up to be different from the young women he had left, a difference signified most immediately by their bobbed hair: "When he went away only little girls wore their hair like that or girls that were fast" (1958, 71). Now, he finds, there are fewer clues to distinguish between "good" girls and "fast" girls. He also fears and rejects the complicated social skills required to "get" a girl; he compares American social relations with the simplicity of relationships with French and German girls, with whom "[y]ou couldn't talk much and you did not need to talk. It was simple and you were friends" (72). The European girls represent relationships not caught up in a dynamic created by war ideology—talking necessitates a negotiation of the ideological definitions that no longer hold true for Krebs. His experience illustrates the confusion that a soldier, educated in gender relationships by pre-war ideology and by his broader education in Europe, felt when returning home to new rules.

The mother/son dynamic, also delineated by pre-war ideology, must now face repercussions caused by the mother's implication in an exploded and repellent system of values and meaning. Krebs's mother has received harsh treatment from critics, who claim that her religious mania and her selfish love prevent her from understanding the needs of her son. Robert Paul Lamb, for example, points to "scenes that seem to demonstrate Mrs. Krebs's unsuitability as a mother" (1995, 25). She is, as propaganda created her, the source of Krebs's patriotism, the mother who embodied the ideals for which he fought and that he has found to be hollow. Yet if Mrs. Krebs is, for Harold, a confining force, it is not her fault. She knows about war, she says, from her father's experience in the Civil War, and if this knowledge is irrelevant to the events of World War I, she is no more ignorant than most soldiers themselves were when they went to war. She tries to reach out to her son: She cooks his breakfast, a gesture of love even if linked to demands that cause feelings of guilt in Krebs; she runs interference with his father to get him access to the car. She recognizes that she cannot ever understand him—that she cannot bridge the gap created by his war experiences. She says that she believes him when he insists that he loves her, but her "all right" indicates more a willingness to allow the fiction that she believes him rather than true belief.

Just as the changes at home confuse soldiers, those same changes also confuse even people who never left. In "Soldier's Home," the war years, in addition to the war itself, have exacerbated tensions between mother and son. Lamb argues that the story has a "larger cultural significance" (1995, 29) than simply the mother-son relationship. He discusses Krebs's reaction to the changes in the girls at home and the social "anxieties, pervasive by the mid-1920s, that the American family . . . was on the verge of collapse" (31). But it is important to connect the two phenomena. Young women experienced a sense of greater freedom during and after the war years, although they did not necessarily have a wider range of choices than their predecessors. If Mrs. Krebs has spent her life defining herself as a wife and mother, she may feel threatened by the bobbed hair and sexual promiscuity that the young women in the story exhibit. The foundations of her domestic life have been rocked by changes that occurred in America while Harold was being changed by the war in Europe.

This chapter addresses the ways the return of the World War I veteran is treated in William Faulkner's *Soldiers' Pay* and Eudora Welty's *Delta Wedding*: how the returning soldier is received by his family and community and how the veteran finds his place within his family. Faulkner's work takes place immediately after the war, while Welty's novel is set a few years later, but both stories explore the impact the First World War had on American domestic life. Faulkner's Donald Mahon, maimed and dying, returns home to fulfill the contract of war, to receive the prize of war ideology: the bride. Joe Gilligan and Welty's George Fairchild, however, recognize the failure of this ideology and instead seek to create a new domestic contract, one that involves a new negotiation of gender.

Faulkner's Return to the Scene of the Crime

William Faulkner's first novel, *Soldiers' Pay*, tells the story of Donald Mahon, a wounded and slowly dying soldier, returning to his father and his fiancée. The title of the novel encapsulates the conflicts arising from the return of soldiers from the First World War to a United States that has continued almost uninterrupted by their absence. Ideally the soldiers are paid with the love of the women they left behind and the respect of their community; in actuality the soldiers were paid with hostility, fear, and resentment. The soldiers themselves pay for their war experiences with the loss of a sense of home and, in the case of Donald and many others, with the loss of life.

Faulkner never fought in the First World War, though he received training as a pilot with the Royal Air Force of Canada. He maintained throughout his life the fiction that he saw combat and passed himself off as an experienced veteran. Critics have speculated on his personal reasons for doing so, but it seems more relevant to consider how his fascination with the war affected his writing. Michael Millgate argues that Faulkner considered the First World War comparable in its effect on its generation to the Civil War: "It became important for him as an artist, perhaps, not so much for its own sake but rather as a source of those permanent truths, those fables of eternal validity, which he saw as inhering in all human conflict" (1974, 103). Faulkner's early work in *Soldiers' Pay* thus prefigures the centrality of war in his later, better known works.[3]

After the First World War, sometime between late 1924 and early 1925, Faulkner wrote a short, unpublished essay called "Literature and War." He concludes the essay with remarks significant to *Soldiers' Pay*: "Who has accused the Anglo-Saxon of being forever sentimental over war? Mankind's emotional gamut is like his auricular gamut: there are some things which he cannot feel, as there are sounds he cannot hear. And war, taken as a whole, is one of these things" (quoted in Millgate 1974, 99). Faulkner's strategy in writing about the war in *Soldiers' Pay* is not to describe battle scenes but to focus on only a part of the soldier's experience: the homecoming. Here Faulkner emphasizes the inability to feel war "as a whole"; Donald Mahon has been wounded in the head, leaving a striking physical and psychological scar and costing him his memory. The other characters all have emotional blind spots related to the war, a deadening of feeling that they know exists in themselves but that they cannot penetrate.

Although the story centers on Donald's return to his home in Charleston, Georgia, the important actions and feelings are those of the people around him. During Donald's train ride home, two people place him under their protection and take upon themselves the responsibility of introducing him into his postwar home. Joe Gilligan is an experienced but not embittered ex-soldier, and Margaret Powers, the widow of a man she married three days before he left for France, is struggling to overcome her feelings of guilt for not loving her husband. Donald's father, a minister, is unable to see his son's inevitably approaching death. Emmy, an unedu-cated woman who was Donald's lover before the war, keeps house for the rector in order to stay close to Donald, whereas Donald's fiancée Cicely Saunders has found a new suitor.

The novel shows a broad spectrum of soldiers embittered by their reception on their return to America and their bewilderment at the changes that have taken place: Joe refers to America as a "foreign coun-try" (Faulkner 1997, 6) that the soldiers must learn to navigate. Many of the civilians express resentment at the sudden influx of ex-soldiers who seem to have no purpose; the train conductor comments that having a trainload of Germans "[c]ouldn't be worse than a train full of you fellows not knowing where you're going" (8). A woman on the train exclaims, "I'm certainly glad my boy wasn't old enough to be a soldier" (15), imply-ing not so much a fear for her son's safety but rather a distaste for what the returning soldiers seem to be. The soldiers, angered by the lack of gratitude for and understanding of their sacrifice and the horrors they have seen, take refuge in alcohol and each other's company as they wan-der vaguely toward their homes. But the soldiers are not completely irre-sponsible and dissolute; confronted with the damaged figure of Donald Mahon, Joe sobers up and takes care of him. Although this gesture is part-ly one of respect toward a fellow soldier who was wounded as Joe himself might have been, it is also a (perhaps unconsciously) selfish one. Joe lacks direction, and the project of returning Donald to his home and allowing him to die in peace gives him a meaningful activity in postwar America.

The returning soldiers are united by their inability to communicate their experiences to the people they left behind. Leed calls silence "the dominant characteristic of veterans of the First World War" (1979, 208); he attributes this silence partly to bitterness, but, as with Harold Krebs and George Campton in Wharton's *Son at the Front*, this silence also stems from the failure of existing language to communicate new experience. Donald says almost nothing in *Soldiers' Pay*, and the narrative breaks into his thoughts only once. Just before he dies, the text reveals Donald's memories of the day he was injured—"a day that had long passed, that had already been spent by those who lived and wept and died, and so remem-bering it, this day was his alone: the one trophy he had reft from Time and Space" (Faulkner 1997, 288–89). His observations of the sky and of his experiences as his body is hit by bullets pass all as moment inside Donald's mind. He looks up, sees his father's face, and tells him, "That's how it happened" (290)—but in fact Donald has explained nothing. The simultaneity of his silent memory and his death signify the impregnability of the soldier's experiences for noncombatants.

Margaret Powers, herself a war veteran, shares with the ex-soldiers a quiet knowledge and a feeling of detachment and displacement from the postwar world. During the war she worked for the Red Cross in New York, and in the excitement of soldiers leaving she married Dick Powers just before he sailed for France. Realizing later that she did not love her husband, Margaret wrote him a letter breaking off the marriage, but he was killed before he received it. Dick's ignorance of her defection and her inability to rectify the situation haunts her and has changed her in ways similar to the soldiers; like them she feels that the world is altered: "Rotten luck. That's exactly what it was, what everything is. Even sorrow is a fake, now" (38). Like Donald, she has an emotional dead spot: "Am I cold by nature, or have I spent all my emotional coppers, that I don't seem to feel things like the others?" (35). Like Joe, she sees helping Donald die in peace as a meaningful occupation; as Stanley Cooperman says, "the expiation, after all, is precisely what sets Margaret apart from the New Woman so incomprehensible to the returning veterans" (1967, 161). This sense of duty and responsibility to the returning Mahon, especially the need to leave him alone, sets Margaret and Joe apart from the small town's inhabitants. Looking into a river at their foreshortened images, Margaret asks, "Do we look that funny to people, I wonder?" (Faulkner 1997, 154) In fact they do; the town speculates in particular about the strange dark woman who returned with Donald Mahon. They can only imagine that she is out to marry Donald or perhaps was his mistress; if they cannot understand the veteran soldiers, they certainly cannot understand the changes the war inflicted on a woman.

The return home is necessarily the return to a woman-centered domesticity. The rector's house seems a safe haven for Donald's recovery and a place for Margaret and Joe to take stock. Margaret finds relief in domestic work, helping Emmy with the dishes and her sewing. The rituals of the home soothe both women: "Steam rose again about Emmy's forearms, wreathing her head, and the china was warm and smooth and sensuous to the touch; glass gleamed under Mrs. Powers' toweling and a dull parade of silver took the light mutely, hushing it as like two priestesses they repeated the orisons of Clothes" (119). Although American society has not provided much comfort for returning soldiers, Joe finds a kind of peace at the rector's house, and he decides to stay on even after Donald's death and Margaret's departure. It is important to note, however, that even though Margaret and Joe find domesticity soothing, neither one has real responsibilities in the Mahon household. Emmy does most of the housework; Margaret participates or not at her own whim. Donald, not Joe, is the son of the family, and so Joe is not subject to the emotional expectations placed on Donald. The rector himself faces the future with a philosophy that anticipates that of Jason Compson III: "The saddest thing about love, Joe, is that not only the love cannot last forever, but even the heartbreak is soon forgotten" (314). What does go on, as he says at the beginning of the novel, is "only unimportant things such as physical comfort: eating and sleeping and procreation" (55). Domesticity, then, is a structure for the continuation of life; it provides rituals that become important because they are enacted.

The return of the soldiers not only brings them into contact with the domestic world but brings the domestic world into contact with the war. The rector calls Joe to help Donald dress because he does not understand his son's military clothing. Even language changes to reflect the influence of soldiers: In his letters to Margaret, Julian Lowe, another ex-soldier, comments that he'd rather be shot than go to tea, but he does go. Even Robert Saunders, Cicely's younger brother who has not been to war, executes "an intricate field maneuver" so that his mother will not see his damaged pants (98). The domestic world is not isolated from the war, even after it is over—military language, clothing, and rituals have infiltrated the home. Civilian life must find a way to include the soldiers and the horror of their experiences.

Home, in *Soldiers' Pay*, is a metaphorical construction as much as it is a physical place. In his essay on the novel, Andrew Scoblionko uses Lacanian ideas to argue that the characters' sense of home is dependent on their ability to manipulate and understand both space and time (1992). Donald, he claims, cannot understand his past and so fails to understand his present; Margaret, in contrast, is always very conscious of her past and thus can create a sense of home wherever she is. I believe, however, that Donald's sense of displacement is due more to his inability to connect whatever vague ideas he has about his present with his understanding of where he *should* be. After being home for several days and visited by old friends, the curious as well as the kind, Donald asks Joe, "When am I going to get out?" and a few minutes later says, "I've got to get home, Joe" (Faulkner 1997, 168). The opacity of Donald's mind hampers the ability to interpret his words. Donald's first comment (i.e., "When am I going to get out?") suggests that he still believes he is in the military, a belief perhaps supported by the constant presence of another military man; Joe seems always to be at Donald's side, ready for the command to "Carry on, Joe." Donald's experience in the war may have destroyed his ability to understand or recognize any other setting. On the other hand, if Donald has any awareness of his current physical location, his comments may be referring to an inability to regard any place as home. Leed describes how soldiers, their idealization of home shattered, attempted to compensate by making their home at the front (as Claude Wheeler does); this "home," however, was perpetually destroyed by the deaths of the members and the continual replacement of those members (1979, 210–12). For the ex-soldier, going home brings with it the difficulties of recognizing home when he sees it; home has become merely a reference point, a place where one used to be safe and comfortable, but his war experiences have forever destroyed his ability to feel safe or comfortable. Home has become a quest, not a place.

In addition to the changes in soldiers' sense of home, *Soldiers' Pay* suggests that in postwar America, gender definitions, which are interdependent with constructions of home, have also changed. Nineteenth-century domestic ideology relied on the idea of the "good woman" who maintained home and cultural values; Faulkner's novel shows a highly conflicted attitude toward this idea of the "good woman." The myth of the war romance also relies on the idea of the "good woman," and corresponding to the destruction of the war romance is the disillusionment with the power of a "good woman." On Donald's return the rector states repeatedly that the "love of a good woman" will be Donald's "best medicine" (Faulkner 1997, 77). When Cicely finally refuses to marry Donald and prepares to leave with George Farr, she first asks Donald's father for forgiveness, saying she is no longer a "good woman" (272). After Donald's death, Emmy, who has refused out of pride to marry him and now regrets it, shows that she too believes in the power of a woman's love: "I would have cured him! If they had just let me marry him instead of [Margaret]!" (292). Yet no woman could have saved Donald; the glorification of the "good woman" turns out to be a powerless construction.

The snakelike presence of Januarius Jones in the rector's house symbolizes the sexual freedom that has infiltrated the traditional system of marriage and domesticity while the soldiers have been away. Michael Zeitlin says of Jones that "he is an incubus in the present, interposing himself between and interfering with personal relations, even as the space he postulates magnetizes the lines of force which hold the group together" (1993, 358). He has free access to the rector's house, and his knowledge of Cicely and George's affair gains him entrance to Cicely's house. He is the sexualized threat—both in his own desire and in his knowledge of the desire of others—within the safe domestic sphere. Jones's existence has in a sense called Cicely into being; she is designed, he thinks, not for motherhood, not for love, but for lust. His repeated attempts at seducing Emmy occur in the rector's house without the rector's knowledge. Emmy, appropriately, fends Jones off with a domestic weapon: a hot iron. Joe's attack on Jones is an attempt to protect the sanctity of the home, but, as the rector says, "Fighting doesn't settle anything" (Faulkner 1997, 312), a comment on the war as well as on Joe's recent skirmish. The ideology of the home will have to incorporate this new, overt sexual element.

Despite the disillusionment about the romance of war, Donald's father and Donald himself still seem to expect the completion of the romantic wartime ideology with the marriage of Donald and Cicely. The doctor who examines Donald sees death in him and asks, "What is he waiting for?": "Something he has begun, but has not completed, something he has carried from his former life that he does not remember consciously. That is his only hold on life that I can see" (150–51). Donald remembers the form of romance—a form in which love counterbalances war—if not Cicely in particular. Cicely is torn between her revulsion at Donald's scar and her desire to fulfill a romantic role as the wife, and soon the widow, of a war hero. When Cicely decides not to place herself in the expected role, Margaret offers herself as Donald's bride. She is aware that Donald must marry someone in order to reach peace. Only with marriage does Donald find release; no longer waiting, he dies. The marriage of the soldier is the completion of the pattern on which the ideology of the war was based; that is, marriage is the compensation he expects for sacrificing his individual identity for the public good.

Margaret's decision to marry Donald suggests the penalty women pay for having participated in the ideology of war and suffering similar disillusionment as the soldiers. Zeitlin's idea of Margaret's "transference of emotion" through which "Mahon is an incarnation of Captain Richard Powers" (1993, 355) helps answer the underlying question and subject of much of the town speculation of whether Margaret loves Donald. Julian Lowe, the young cadet who, like Faulkner, never got to fly in battle, believes she is in love with Donald, "knowing that if he were a woman, he would be" (Faulkner 1997, 48). Julian believes in the unconquerable power of a fighter pilot's ability to win women's hearts. But Margaret's own thoughts on the issue are more complicated: "Oh yes, I'm in love with him! I'd like to hold his poor ruined head against my breast and not let him wake again ever. . . . Oh, hell, what a mess it all is!" (79) Her language recalls previous incidents when she has held Julian's head against her breast as she will later hold the rector's. Her love is largely maternal, and with Donald she longs for the ability to relieve him of the burden of the life he has returned to. Faced with the true, unmixed grief of a mother whose son died in the war, Margaret denies having lost anyone she loved (254). Having denied love for Dick, the feelings she transfers to Donald are not love but rather guilt and responsibility. Love, for

Margaret, has become too complicated by the ideology of war; when she
admits to feelings for Joe, she does so only on the grounds that they not
marry and instead leave each other free to end the relationship at any
time.

Margaret stands in contrast to the other women the men left behind,
shallow women the soldiers cannot understand. Part of this problem is the
women's lack of knowledge about the war. Cooperman discusses the difference a few years makes between the two groups of young people; unlike
the men who went to war, the postwar youth were "[y]oung people for
whom the war served chiefly as a means to achieve social and sexual
emancipation" (1967, 161). At the dance the young people are described
as "[b]oys of both sexes" (Faulkner 1997, 186); women have cut their hair
and changed their clothing, indicating a new manifestation of femininity. Women no longer wear corsets but rather flimsy dresses; as several people comment about Cicely, "you can see right through her" (201, 204–5).
This remark comments on Cicely's shallow personality as much as it does
on her dress.

These new young women represent most sharply the difference in values between those who have gone to war and those who have not. Julian
Lowe becomes disillusioned about the young women at home, writing to
Margaret that "[g]irls are not like you they are so young and dumb you cant
trust them" (242). Joe predicts even before meeting Cicely that she will
refuse to marry Donald, basing his knowledge on a letter of Cicely's that
contains "all the old bunk about knights of the air and the romance of battle" (36–37). Cicely is described as "a flower stalk or a young tree relaxed
against the table: there was something so fragile, so impermanent since
robustness and strength were unnecessary, yet strong withal as a poplar is
strong through very absence of strength, about her" (76). Cicely lacks
Margaret's strength in action and of will, yet she holds sexual power over
the young men she knows. This strength in negativity has not prepared
her to face the unpleasantness of life that war both is and represents. For
the soldiers the romance of battle has been gone for some time, and
Donald's body bears the marks of the reality of war. Cicely screams and
faints at the sight of Donald, at the reality that does not fit into her
knowledge of the world.

But it is too easy to dismiss Cicely as manipulative and morally weak.
Despite the charges that she is a shallow, cold-hearted flirt,[4] Cicely shows
the disparity between the postwar woman's freedom and the actuality of her
choices. Her character shows the weakness of the society that created her.
She tries to imagine options other than traditional marriage for herself:
"How would I like to have a husband and a wife? Or two husbands? I wonder if I want to get married at all" (80). She shocks her lover George Farr

by commenting that since they have had sex they no longer need to be married, but her sexual freedom has actually trapped her. She deeply resents the fact that she will have a baby. Despite her questioning of traditional expectations, she is still left with marriage as her only practical option.

Soldiers' Pay shows conflicting attitudes toward the American home and domesticity, attitudes divided along gender lines. Women's restlessness with their role as housekeepers and mothers has increased; Cicely's internal rebellion against marriage shows the changes in women's expectations. For Margaret and Joe, the oppression of the home remains a dividing obstacle. Margaret asks Joe to come with her, unmarried, so "when we get fed up all we need do is wish each other luck and go our separate ways" (303). Her objection to marriage is grounded not so much in her sexual experiences as in her knowledge of the cultural implications of marriage—her fear that, as with her first husband, she will come to symbolize more than she can be. To Joe, Margaret comments that the keeping of her "good name" is men's problem, not hers: "What you mean by a good name is like a dress that's too flimsy to wear comfortably" (101). The reference to a "flimsy dress" oddly anticipates Cicely and her see-through party dress, Cicely who decides to maintain her good name by marrying George. Margaret's proposal to Joe echoes Cicely's comment to George that they do not need to get married; both women hesitate to commit themselves to an institution that they know will limit their opportunities and their control over their bodies. Despite her promiscuity and New Woman rebelliousness, it is Cicely who cannot evade the confines of marriage; Margaret's experience with the war has provided her with the strength to carry through what Cicely cannot. For both women it is their men who insist on marriage; Cicely is caught whereas Margaret escapes—at an emotional cost that is only suggested.

Joe, on the other hand, finds comfort in the rector's house and the prospect of continuing on in a filial relationship to Donald's father. For him, domesticity has turned out to have more rewards than restrictions. Perhaps the reverend's house reminds him of the routines of the military; it is, after all, a mostly male household. Joe finds a kindly father figure, one who has already lost his son and who thus has no more expectations to place on Joe.

Soldiers' Pay offers no easy solutions for the reincorporation of soldiers into their families; it suggests, in fact, that the approximation of home is the best a soldier can hope for. The ideology of home and war that sent the soldiers to battle falls apart, and Faulkner indicates that for men and women both there is no replacement. His is not a hopeless novel, but it does demonstrate that the war has done permanent damage. The war—men's experience of it and women's inability to understand it—has divided the sexes yet again; even the women who have experienced it are separated from men by changed feelings toward marriage and sexuality.

The War-Defined Family in *Delta Wedding*

Eudora Welty wrote her 1945 novel *Delta Wedding* during the Second World War. The novel started out as a short story, "The Delta Cousins," but became a novel at the suggestion of Welty's editor, Diarmuid Russell. Critics have focused on Welty's trips to the Delta to visit her friend John Robinson and on Welty's own childhood memories as sources for the novel,[5] but World War II is an important influence behind the more obvious sources. Suzanne Marrs speculates that during this time Welty's "thoughts were with Robinson, stationed in Europe as an intelligence officer with the Army Air Corps" (1993, 79), and Welty also had brothers in the war. Although Welty was criticized by reviewers such as Diana Trilling in 1943 for writing about myths and dreams in her collection *The Wide Net*, Albert J. Devlin, in his essay "The Making of *Delta Wedding*," argues that "fantasy was precisely [Welty's] way of entering modern history" (1996, 251) and that writing the novel was her response to the bombing of Pearl Harbor (ibid., 252). To view *Delta Wedding* as a war novel is to understand Welty's artistic vision of placing the political in the personal. I have chosen this novel as the last one examined in this book because it brings us full circle, back to the domestic novel that incorporates, encircles, and helps define the war novel. In *Delta Wedding*, Welty portrays the aftereffects of war on the structure and gender roles of an American family.

Delta Wedding is set in the South in 1923, only a few years after the end of World War I. Nine-year-old Laura McRaven arrives at Shellmound, the Fairchild plantation, as the family prepares for the wedding of the second daughter, Dabney, to the overseer, Troy Flavin. Laura's uncle Battle and his wife Ellen are at the center of Fairchild life, with eight children and another on the way. Dabney's older sister Shelley prepares for a trip to Europe, and the family faces a crisis in the possible split between Battle's brother George and his wife Robbie over George's saving his niece Maureen from an oncoming train. The novel describes the rhythms of Fairchild family life, heightened by the upcoming event: family members arriving, visits to homes of great-aunts, cooking, cleaning, and anticipation. The story is told from the point of view of seven Fairchild women: Laura, Ellen, Robbie, Dabney, Shelley, India (Laura's nine-year-old cousin), and Tempe (Battle's older sister). Each woman's perspective is affected by her generation, her relationship with the male members of the family, and her place within the domestic sphere.

Critics have focused on the apparent lack of plot in the novel. In her 1946 review Diana Trilling writes: "Dramatically speaking, nothing happens in 'Delta Wedding'" (1994, 103). Welty herself has said that she went to a great deal of trouble to set the novel in a year in which nothing happened—"in which all the men could be home and uninvolved. It couldn't be a war year. It couldn't be a year when there was a flood in the Delta. . . . It had to be a year that would leave my characters all free to have a family story" (Bunting 1984, 49). Many critics have quoted Welty and challenged the notion that "nothing happens" in the novel; as John Crowe Ransom points out, *Delta Wedding*, like other novels, "is like an epic in that the individual actions are seen against the background of the cultus, the social establishment" (1989, 71). Romines and Levy, both discussing domestic writing, argue that on the contrary a great deal "happens"; there is much to be read in Welty's focus on the symbolic work of housekeeping. Through activities such as cooking and caring for domestic objects, Romines argues, the Fairchild women reveal their thoughts and anxieties about family relationships, sexuality, and race relations (1997). The imminent wedding, according to Romines, is an event that heightens the importance of domestic activities—a ritual that allows the women to exhibit their skills and reinscribes the importance of home and family tradition.

It is useful to recognize further that 1923 is *not*, for the Fairchild family, a year when all of the men are "home and uninvolved." One man in particular is missing and will never return home: Denis Fairchild, killed in the First World War. Even though *Delta Wedding* is the story of a family's daily life and its reproduction of itself with the new couple of Dabney and Troy, it is also a tale of mourning—for Laura's mother, Annie Laurie, but also for the dead Denis. The novel can be read as the story of a family's coming to terms with the death of one of its men in war and the reincorporation of another member, George Fairchild, into the family system. To say 1923 is a year in which nothing happened may be true, but outside events such as the First World War have repercussions that last, sometimes almost imperceptibly. Romines, speaking of Shelley's encounter with the violence of the men's world at the overseer's office, argues that behind the domestic story are "worlds that *Delta Wedding* does not explore but that are always *present* in close and tense relation to the intimately rendered world of women's culture" (1997, 216); in addition to the issues of class and race that critics such as Romines discuss,[6] the novel also reflects the impact of the First World War on domestic life. Despite Welty's claim to have wanted to write just a "family story," *Delta Wedding* is a war story as well—the separation is not always possible.

Like the Drakes of Bailey's *Tin Soldier*, war is not a new phenomenon for the Fairchilds, and much of the family history revolves around war stories; in *Delta Wedding*, however, the war stories are those of the women. Ransom comments that the "preponderance of females" in the novel is "lucky for the special grade of communication that has to be made to the reader" (1989, 72), as if the reason the women outnumber the men is a convenient way for Welty to create a certain message. A closer look reveals that the absence of men is not simply a fortuitous plot device: Many of the older Fairchild women are war widows. Losing husbands in war has become a fact of life for these women. When Dabney visits her aunts Primrose and Jim Allen to tell them about her engagement, the aunts recite part of the family history, the list of soldiers who died in the Civil War: "[Uncle George's] brother Battle was killed and his brother Gordon was killed, and Aunt Shannon's husband Lucian Miles killed and Aunt Maureen's husband Duncan Laws" (Welty 1982, 57). Aunt Mac and Aunt Shannon continue to compete with each other over who misses her husband more. According to family legend, the older Uncle George's wife Mashula "waited for him to come home from the Civil War till the lightning one early morning stamped her picture on the window-pane" (ibid.). Uncle George never did return, and the night light Mashula sat with is passed down to Dabney, the bride-to-be, suggesting a tradition of women linked by their waiting for men to come home from war.

Fairchild life—its objects and rituals—incorporates war and death into daily experience. Mashula's lamp itself integrates violence into domesticity because when it is lit "you saw a redness glow and the little town was all on fire, even to the motion of fire" (58–59); the image of the burning town recalls propaganda pictures of Belgian towns set on fire by German soldiers (or even homes burned in the U.S. South during Sherman's march). The main Fairchild house Shellmound is filled with "Somebody's gun," "Somebody's pistol," and "Somebody's fowling piece he left behind him when he marched off to Mexico, never to be laid eyes on again. There were the Civil War muskets Aunt Mac watched over, an old Minie rifle coming to pieces before people's eyes" (130). The relics and weapons from these wars both decorate the Fairchild homes and are sources of stories, wonder, and entertainment. War is part of the history on which the Fairchild myth of family[7] sustains itself.

A more general sense of violence pervades Fairchild family life. Louise Westling argues that on a basic level *Delta Wedding* reminds readers that death and violence are inherent in daily life; in her discussion of the continual presence of food in the novel she points out that "[t]o eat is to feed off death, to be part of the mystery that includes reproduction, growth, ultimate decay and regeneration" (1992, 34).[8] Furthermore, the language of violence is the medium through which family members relate to each other: "They spoke of killing and whipping in the exasperation and help-lessness of much love" (Welty 1982, 25). The children are violent toward each other, both in what they say and what they do, and this violence is the counterbalance to their love; Maureen, Laura realizes, is really most-ly gentle and only sometimes violent. The love of the adults for the chil-dren is often expressed in terms of violence as well. Battle talks of skinning the children alive (152), and it is when he hits Laura's and India's legs with a stick as punishment and refers to them both as "[a] man's daughters!" (237) that Laura learns she is to be a flower girl and feels truly part of the family.

In the postwar years, the novel suggests, women have to pay a price for the loss of the men in war. Part of that price is bearing children. Nancy Huston answers the question of why men fight with the answer that "men make war *because* women have children" (1986, 119); men, she suggests, have needed to find an important and sacred activity equivalent to women's ability to give birth. In *Delta Wedding,* however, the situation is the reverse: Women have children because men have died in war. Ellen Fairchild is in the midst of her tenth pregnancy; because her brother-in-law Denis is dead, Ellen must ensure the continuation and the expansion of the family Denis died for, at the risk of her own life. Several times the novel links pregnancy with death;[9] for example, the comedy of errors that Ellen recites about her first pregnancy, with both her mother and the doc-tor passed out on the floor, could easily have been a tragedy. The same doctor later tells Shelley, "Tell your mother to call a halt. She'll go here," referring to a plot in the cemetery (Welty 1982, 177) and thus connect-ing childbirth with death. The novel hints in other places that this preg-nancy will be too much for Ellen: her fainting; the bird in the house that portends death; Shelley's referral to pregnancy as a "predicament"; and finally Ellen's wondering "what would happen to everything if she were not here to watch it, . . . not for the first time when a child was coming" (297–98). Although the novel does not imply that Ellen's death in child-birth is inevitable, the danger she faces is real.

Perhaps because so many Fairchild men have died in war, the women of the family treasure those who remain; it has become the women's role to glorify the men. Denis is always in the background as an ideal, and ref-erences to him are usually coupled with the comment that he was killed in the war or that he was the sweetest man ever born in the Delta. Aunt Tempe in particular "stated it like a fact of the weather, that it was Denis and always would be Denis that they gave the family honor to":

Denis was the one that looked like a Greek god, Denis who squandered away his life loving people too much, was too kind to his family, was torn to pieces by other people's misfortune, married beneath him, threw himself away in drink, got himself killed in the war. . . . It was Denis who had read everything in the world and had the prodigious memory—not a word ever left him. Denis knew law, and could have told you the way Mississippi could be made the fairest place on earth to live, all of it like the Delta. It was Denis that was ahead of his time and it was Denis that was out of the pages of a book too. . . . Denis could have been anything and done everything, but he was cut off before his time. (152–53).

As the preceding passage suggests, Denis was not perfect: He was a womanizer, a gambler, a drinker. His death in the war has relieved him of the burdens of being a human man in the Fairchild family and allows them to forget that he married "beneath" him; as a dead war hero he is the standard for the other men and the expected object of reverence for the rest of the Fairchilds. George, a war veteran, receives similar homage, although always to a lesser degree than Denis (Tempe demands of Robbie: "*Why* have you treated George Fairchild the way you have? . . . Except for Denis Fairchild, the sweetest man ever born in the Delta?" [207]), but Battle, who did not go to war at all, is never referred to in such terms. The family hierarchy of honor corresponds to how near the men came to death in war—and consequently how much they sacrificed for the women.

With Denis dead, the family does not have to face the changes the war may have caused in him; he maintains a "pure, unvarying glory" (82). His drinking, womanizing, and gambling have become mere footnotes to his character, although it is possible that the war would have only exacerbated these characteristics. As we have seen with other returning soldiers—Krebs, Mahon, and Gilligan—men who participated in the First World War are profoundly affected by its horrors and impersonality to the extent that family members can often no longer understand them.

For George Fairchild, returning from the war poses such problems. He has seen the death and destruction inflicted by impersonal technological warfare, and he has been wounded, physically and emotionally. He is not, like Mahon, permanently damaged; he sees life, though changed, as still livable—unlike, in *One of Ours*, the returning soldiers Mrs. Wheeler reads about who "leave prematurely the world they have come back to" (370). But he must negotiate the demands of his family, who seem to have little understanding of or desire to understand his experiences in war. George has always been more aware than his brother Denis of the broader world around him, as Dabney's memory of George's interference in a fight between two African American boys shows: Coming upon the boys fighting with a knife, Denis runs off into the woods, laughing, while

George breaks up the fight and binds the wounds of the injured boy (43–44). Dabney's reaction to this scene typifies the exclusive claim the Fairchilds believe they have on George: "[A]ll the Fairchild in her had screamed at his interfering—at his taking part—*caring* about anything in the world but them" (46). George's war experiences have changed him and further separated him from the family. Before the war he farmed at the plantation; he has since become a lawyer living in Memphis. He came home from the war, "a lonely man that noticed wildflowers" (280), and now, unlike the rest of the family, "he saw death on its way" (248). More important, he does not fear death, claiming that "I don't think it matters what *happens* to a person, or what comes. . . . To *me!* I speak for myself" (246). The distinction between himself and other Fairchilds seems to have always existed but perhaps was made clearer to him by the war. Having seen death on a large scale, his attitude toward it reveals a sensibility different from that of the other Fairchilds: a sense of the larger world, its fragility, its impersonality, and the responsibility it demands from an individual.

For this reason George seems to have a special relationship with his brother's wife, Ellen. Ellen, a Virginian, is an outsider and yet the center of the Fairchild family—a dual role that George fills as well. Figuratively, too, they match as a pair in Huston's "matrix of war": Ellen the child-bearer, George the soldier.[10] Ellen's consciousness, which reaches moments of epiphany and knowing throughout the novel, seems to be able to reach into that of others, especially George. She acknowledges his complexities as the rest of the family refuses to do: "[S]he thought that she could tell . . . that he was more remarkable than either ["the family's hero or sacrificial beast"], and not owing to Denis's spectacular life or death, but to his being in himself all that Denis no longer was, a human being and a complex man" (82). Ellen can talk to George, as we do not see her talk to her husband; she tells George about the girl in the woods and responds without judgment to his confession of having slept with her. George, in turn, protects Ellen, seeing that the laughing parade of children chasing the bird is too much for her and reviving her when she faints. At the dance after the wedding, George makes her feel "lucky—cherished, and somehow *pretty* (which she knew she never was)" (298), and Ellen speculates "as the waltz played and they moved by a tree where a golden lantern hung, and without one regret for her life with Battle, she might have been the one" (294)—"the one who relieved the heart's overflow" (293). But Ellen's flashes of insight also indicate her inability to understand George. Her flashes are just that—brief bursts of understanding that are not always corroborated by other sources. She "might have been the one," but she is not.

As it is, Ellen is one of the primary makers of the family myth that George finds so entrapping.[11] She recognizes, however, that Robbie may provide something for George that the family cannot: "They're both as direct as two blows on the head of a nail, George and Robbie, Ellen was thinking" (150). Robbie's directness is probably a welcome relief for George from the subtle pressures and expectations the Fairchild women place on him. Robbie, thinking of the Fairchilds, views them as somehow divided, with an inner core "like a burning string in a candle" (208), and thus separated between words and feelings, outer and inner. Robbie, in contrast, views herself as whole—she just feels, and her words reflect her feelings directly. She believes that only she can save George from the family: "Only she could hold him against that grasp, that separating thrust of Fairchild love that would go on and on" (195). George, as critics such as Joseph Childers argue, must walk a tightrope between the demands of his family and the demands of his marriage, but he needs the counterbalance of Robbie to allow him to negotiate the complex web of family expectation.

George knows that the world is changing and that the Fairchilds' way of life will change with it. Through Robbie's consciousness we learn that their apartment in Memphis contains all new furniture rather than the family heirlooms of the other Fairchild houses. Although the Fairchild women and even some critics blame the decorating on Robbie, the newness and isolation of their apartment is not merely the influence of the lower-class woman; Robbie "knew [a matching bedroom set] would please George, new and shiny and expensive" (182). Though he talks of returning to the Delta to farm, George is a city man, a lawyer, a representative of the new. In his review of the novel, Ransom comments that "the pattern of Southern life as Miss Welty has it is doomed" (1989, 74), and Welty agrees with this assessment: "I think that was implicit in the novel: that this was all such a fragile, temporary thing. At least I hope it was. That's why I searched so hard to find the year in which that could be most evident. Well, you're living in a very precarious world without knowing it, always" (Bunting 1984, 50). Most of the Fairchilds do not seem to know that they live in a precarious world; no one mentions the particulars of Denis's or George's experiences in the war, only the fact of Denis's death. George, on the other hand, has a deeper understanding of social change. Marrs argues that unlike other Fairchilds, "George reveres those who can face the unknown with courage and serenity," referring to George's appreciation of his pioneer ancestors (1993, 88); this reverence, I believe, comes at least partly through George's experience in the war— the acquisition of a Hemingway herolike serenity.

The Fairchilds seem either to ignore or to be unaware of the changes in American life. Ellen's continual pregnancies illustrate this refusal or inability to see; Ellen herself thinks, "sometimes now the whole world seemed rampant, running away from her, and she would always be carrying another child to bring into it" (Welty 1982, 102). Ellen, and perhaps other Fairchilds, sense change, but they fail to understand it and so respond to it poorly or not at all. The fertility that Westling sees as glorified in the novel[12] can also be viewed as dangerous. The large number of Fairchilds is itself a threat in the modern world—not only to Ellen's life, but to the Fairchild way of life. In the previous generation there are also a large number of children: Battle, Denis, George, Tempe, Rowena, Primrose, Jim Allen, and Annie Laurie. But only two of those women married, one of whom died; of the men, Denis is dead, and only Battle has a family (though the text hints that George's wife Robbie may be pregnant). Thus far the family land has remained consolidated, but with Battle and Ellen's children starting to come of age and marry, it will be increasingly difficult to find homes for them all on Shellmound land. In the near future family members will inevitably disperse. The Fairchild silver goblets exemplify this point; as Troy polishes each one, Ellen tells him which child each cup will go to: "We have so many daughters—of course you have to divide things up" (122). Only a few family members welcome change: On the trestle, Maureen reaches out to embrace the oncoming train (115); similarly, at the end of the novel Laura holds "both arms . . . out to the radiant night" (326). Maureen's embrace becomes unnecessary by the miracle of the train's ability to stop, but Laura's embrace of the oncoming world—a world about which she seems to know more than many of her relatives—suggests that the world cannot be stopped. Even the secluded privacy of Shellmound cannot keep it out.

Yet, as Sharlee Glenn argues, the physical dispersal of the family does not necessarily mean the family will be destroyed. The domestic rituals established by Ellen and the aunts will be carried on by the daughters and granddaughters. And George, with his insight into the changing world, can help his family survive: "By shocking his family into an awareness of the individual—by helping them see the clan as a group of separate, divergent free agents who have their own personal, private lives and who can act and react in individual ways without threat to the group, George prepares his family for the social change that is coming" (1989, 58). Dr. Murdoch says George is not a "family man," but hints that Robbie is pregnant meaning that George may become a father. It seems clear, though, that he will not be a "family man" in the way that his brother Battle is. Battle, with such a large family, seems to find refuge in loving his children, as Shelley notes, "by the bunch," whereas George takes his family "one by one" (Welty 1982, 110). George, should he have children, would most likely have fewer children than Battle—as an ex-soldier he is probably well versed in birth control[13]—and would love his children with more attention to them individually.

George's marriage to Robbie signals the changes that the war has inflicted on the American social structure. His marrying outside of his class inspires new thinking from Dabney: "It was actually Uncle George who had shown her that there was another way to be—something else" (42)—a sense that the world is different and that she has different choices. Dabney chooses, like George, to marry "beneath" her, and she hopes to make a new way of life as a married woman. She views marriage as an escape from loneliness, expecting Troy to provide for her the strength to walk in the night with "a woman's serious foot" (119). Welty does not necessarily indicate that Dabney can create the married life she desires, however. We see Troy's expectations that Dabney will be a traditional, submissive wife; when they receive his mother's quilts as a wedding present, he tells her "to fold them nice, Dabney" (149), and after their wedding trip he hushes her ungenerous comment with a rebuke: "Shame on you, pussy" (325). Partheny, the black nurse who bakes a cake that supposedly has the power to restore Robbie to George, tells Shelley and India, "I goin' to bring Miss Dab heart-shape patticake of her own—come de time" (172), suggesting, like the great-aunts' gift of a lamp, that Dabney will have marital problems. Danielle Fuller argues that the women in the novel are, despite the appearance of a matriarchy, enmeshed in a highly patriarchal system and that they "are forced to manoeuvre between the roles available to them and their own imaginative impulses and desires" (1994, 293). Even two-year old Bluet, whose legs want "to kick like a dancer's" when she sleeps, works during the day "like a busy housewife" (Welty 1982, 83), suggesting the perpetual suppression of women's creative impulses by the patriarchal system of heterosexuality and marriage. Although men like George may be able to make a break, Dabney's choice to marry and remain on the Fairchild plantation suggests that she may be in for a more difficult battle than she anticipates.

Dabney's older sister Shelley seems to be imagining a different life for herself, a life resistant to the domestic rituals of her female relatives. She says she will never marry, smokes cigarettes, reads the latest books, and drives a car. Romines claims that "[i]t is [Shelley] most especially who puts Fairchild life in a wider context," comparing her to other modern women such as Daisy Buchanan and Brett Ashley (1997, 215). Like Daisy and Brett, Shelley is associated with the exciting and exotic world of Europe. But, as Fuller argues, "even Shelley realises that her trip to Europe is a temporary removal from Shellmound conducted according to male rules" (1994, 302–3); she is, after all, chaperoned by the imperious Tempe, who is one of the primary enforcers of heterosexual conduct in the novel. *Delta Wedding* suggests that women who leave the plantation come to no good end: Laura's mother, Annie Laurie, died; Aunt Tempe's daughter seems to have made an unfortunate marriage to a Yankee; even the strange girl in the woods is seduced by George and later killed by a train. Shelley's future may be filled with new possibilities, but she also faces the role played by so many of her aunts: the spinster.

Delta Wedding presupposes an impending modernist sense of loss and isolation—a loneliness already present in the individual characters themselves and brought out by the domestic life of the family. In her diary Shelley writes, "I think one by one we're all more lonely than private and more lonely than self-sufficient" (Welty 1982, 110). Ellen sees the complexities and isolation of the everyday: "what caves were in the mountains, what blocked chambers, and what crystal rivers that had not yet seen light" (206). She sees her son Ranny, for example, "riding the horse of his mind" (106), alone in his own world. M. E. Bradford suggests that the "dozen small rebellions" occurring in the novel are included "to demonstrate how well they are contained" within the family (1979, 203), but I think rather the point of these "rebellions" is to suggest the inability of the family to contain them and the impossibility of trying. Domestic rituals perpetuate the family myth but also provide a frame for rebellion, as baking a cake creates time for Ellen to think about the possibilities of her life and that of her daughters. Shelley, furthermore, realizes that George does not protest against "the hiding and protesting that went on, the secrecy of life" (Welty 1982, 255); George's quiet acceptance of the "secrecy of life" within the domestic frame is one of the qualities that makes him so dear to the other Fairchilds.

Despite the novel's emphasis on the characters' isolation, Welty also suggests that that isolation can be alleviated. Ellen has one flash of communion with George, one moment when she senses that she is not alone. When she reveals to George that she has met a girl in the woods and he responds that he too has met her, Ellen is "speechless": "It was a thing [Ellen] had never learned in her life, to expect that what has come to you, come in dignity to yourself in loneliness, will yet be shared, the secret never intact" (103). The mysteries of daily life, the caves and rivers, can sometimes be not only sensed but also shared. The moment is always ephemeral, never expected, but its very existence, even once, leaves Ellen simultaneously aware of the possibilities of human relationships and respectful of life's secrets.

In *Delta Wedding* we see the consequences of the war for an American family. War has brought about change in class consciousness, which can be seen in George's and Dabney's marriages. Home life, however, is still problematic, as it still threatens women with suffocation and death. "The double helix" and "the matrix of war" have their impact on women. Although it seems that women have new options, underneath these possibilities their lives are still severely restricted. Significantly, India suggests that Ellen's baby will be named after Denis, the figure who, as an idealized hero, perpetuates a rigid gender system and a belief in the supremacy of family, rather than after George, the soldier who has returned and changed. Many critics argue that George will return to the Shellmound plantation, yet his discussion of such a return at the end of the novel seems more idle talk, a teasing fantasy that George knows he will not carry out. Rather, he and Robbie will continue to negotiate their demands on each other and to offer a domestic model that is different from the one Shellmound provides.

Conclusion

Neither Welty nor Faulkner provides an alternative to American domesticity founded on violence and war; rather, both writers describe ideological clashes between veterans and civilians, conflicts that engage definitions of home, domesticity, and gender. The home becomes a testing ground on which and for which ideological battles are waged. For women, social roles have seemed to expand—Cecily's experimental attitude toward sexuality, Margaret's proposal of a relationship without marriage, Shelley's association with modern American life—yet all of these women are still limited in their choices by forces that underlie the very framework of choice. As the nation recovers from war and from ideological disruptions that threaten men's sense of self, women are commandeered to help reestablish the power and superiority of masculinity.

If, as Gilbert and Gubar (1988) argue, the early twentieth century is a battleground between the sexes for control over the literary terrain, the topic of the returning soldier is one over which both sides can claim authority. The veteran himself cannot be viewed in a vacuum but rather, as both Faulkner and Welty show, within the context of the American home. Domesticity, in fact, has a place for both dead soldiers and veterans, although veterans and their families may struggle to define this role. The reincorporation of soldiers into American homes is crucial for writers in understanding the role of the United States in the First World War and the war's effect on American society.

Conclusion

The selection of writers examined here—of both sexes, of different generations, of the literary establishment and of popular appeal, of modernists and realists—offers a much larger picture of World War I and its range of issues than any one of these single authors could provide. Taken as a whole, these texts represent a compelling arc of ideas that evolved over the course of the United States' participation in the war. Early texts established the ideological system of gender, a structure that produced roles for men and women in relation to the war and that sought to equate the value of gendered work, and those same works suggested the problems inherent in that system. Later texts exposed these difficulties and inconsistencies more openly as people experienced the war and had time to reflect on it; these novels respond directly to the ideas set forth in earlier works. This arc of the development of a war ideology and of reactions to it shows that the domestic world and World War I are inextricably interlinked.

In concluding her study *The Home Plot*, Ann Romines states that "domestic life is not alien to and hidden from . . . public life, not a dirty little secret that housekeepers share" (1992, 293). Home is a powerful, compelling construct, and the rituals that it requires and evokes make profound statements about the social, political, and emotional needs of the people who exist in it. Home defines and is defined by its social and political context and is, as Ellen Glasgow's David Blackburn insists, the place of formation for individuals. The mindset for war, for example, originates long before boys leave for boot camp; it begins when they absorb idealized notions from the family, especially mothers, about what men do in battle and about their relationship to the nation. Like Temple Bailey's Derry Drake and Eudora Welty's Shellmound men, they often recognize their place amidst a long line of soldiers who have been revered in family legend. Girls, similarly, learn that their responsibility is to take care of their men physically, emotionally, and—perhaps most important—ideologically, as Jean McKenzie discovers she must let her husband go to war in order for them both to take their places in the adult world. The ideology that informs and constructs the home must be continually examined, and a close study of domestic literature reveals that the structures of the home are quite complicated.

Though often perceived as a place of safety and security, the home is not as sheltering as it may at first seem. Violence, often unobtrusively, is bred in the home through the system of Western family dynamics, and it is an organized violence that can feed into the ideology of war. Cather's Claude Wheeler, for example, learns that to be a man he must participate in a regulated arrangement of violence: the military. In times of war, the ideology that constructs the home cannot avoid its implication with an ideology of war, and because of this interdependency, women's domestic novels necessarily tell us much about social attitudes toward war.

War literature demonstrates that the emotional demand for a home is ungendered, although gender inscribes men's and women's roles in relation to that home. With the gendering of the home comes a value inscription by which the home becomes secondary to whatever world is defined as "masculine," whether it be business or war, and the sense of hierarchy that comes with this gendering produces problems for men thrown into a new relationship to the domestic. War novels indicate that men need an idea of home—whether it is the memory of a home left behind or the presence of a physical place and the creation of domestic rituals at the battle front—just as much as women do. The domestic is the known, defined, and predictable; war is the unknown, unexpected, and unpredictable. Domestic rituals fulfill human needs for meaning, security, and a sense of belonging, and literature reflects these needs. During war, soldiers attempt to establish the security of the home by re-creating its rituals.

The experience of war brings soldiers to disillusionment with the home and the home front because the ideals that have been instilled in them so thoroughly have been proven false or hollow. Soldiers cannot escape the rituals through which the home operates, however. Rather, they reproduce them. War texts, though often intending to show disillusionment with society (figured as feminine, through individual wives and especially mothers but also through the feminization of the home front itself), nevertheless include portrayals of domestic rituals. These descriptions sometimes reveal a desire for the home and its comforting familiarity but can also function as signifiers of change. Meals in John Dos Passos's *Three Soldiers* and Thomas Boyd's *Through the Wheat*, for example, are in themselves indicators of the corruption of the nation that sent the soldiers to war and of the military that controls them. Just as in domestic novels, domestic ritual comments on the nature of the larger society to which the characters belong.

While soldiers' idealized notions of the domestic world are shattered by the reality of war, other sacred ideals are also threatened. At the battle front of World War I, soldiers were shocked to discover that the U.S. military held no respect for the ideals of Americanness—that is, of independence and autonomy. Mechanized warfare offered no rewards for individual action and instead required that the soldier submit his will to that of the nation. Domestic rituals, already emotionally necessary in peacetime, became also for some soldiers a means to resist the loss of identity in war; in Dos Passos's *One Man's Initiation* two officers ritualize their meal to prevent becoming mere parts of a machine. The battle front of World War I literature is not only a horror of bullets, shells, and gas but also a place where rituals of identity occur, groups bond, and the reproduction of home activities offers comfort.

Because of the feminization of the home and the nation during World War I, women as individuals—and as writers, especially in the case of Cather, but also of Wharton and others—and as a group became objects of scorn and bitterness. Yet the rejection of the feminine left soldiers in a double bind. Many soldiers recognized that they themselves had become feminized during the war because of the enforced passivity of trench warfare and their submission to an unseen military hierarchy. Ironically, instead of proving their manhood, the First World War stripped them of it. Even though women became handy targets for soldiers' animosity, underlying soldiers' resentment of women is anger at the nation's technique of transferring them from one system of values to another—from a world where skill in killing is valued and actual or potential death is accepted and honored, to a world where killing is abhorrent and no one wants to think about death.

Women, particularly those who had hoped to make social and political gains through their support of the First World War, found instead that their investment in the war cost them the respect of the very soldiers they encouraged. They had participated in the war, actually and ideologically, with the understanding that their backing was necessary to the soldiers, and instead of being rewarded for their sacrifices, women were resented by veterans and unable to comprehend their experiences and resulting psychological trauma. Furthermore, women were forced to cope with returning soldiers, who became yet another element of disorder that the housekeeper must contain and incorporate into her household system. Welty's Tempe, for example, makes her brother George into a comprehensible and orderly element by establishing his place in the family hierarchy and attempting to regulate his own marital and domestic arrangements. For younger women the war years seemed to offer greater freedom, but the structures that forced the men back into an understandable social ingredient conscripted these women into their service.

Through literature, the experience of war becomes incorporated into the American sense of identity and daily life, even if the country is not currently engaged in war. Literature has the power to influence national character and purpose even if the current generation has personally never experienced war. Crane's *Red Badge of Courage* taught (if misleadingly) boys what war was like, and thus knowledge—actual or imagined—of the Civil War shaped the experience of World War I by shattering soldiers' expectations and sowing distrust between the soldiers and the United States. The repercussions of this misapplication shaped the writers of World War I, with a resulting rejection of the national sensibility that produced such texts and with a consequent desire to undermine existing literary modes. This cycle repeats itself through U.S. history, as soldiers who had World War I as a model went to World War II, and those with World War II went to Vietnam. Ernest Hemingway recognized this cycle and the way in which it handicapped soldiers, and in an attempt to prepare young men for World War II, he edited a collection of war stories, titled *Men at War,* to prepare soldiers for World War II. In World War I, Hemingway learned that "nothing could happen to me that had not happened to all men before me. Whatever I had to do men had always done. If they had done it then I could do it too and the best thing was not to worry about it" (1968, 6). Yet, by definition a war novel requires a soldier's rejection of the established culture—not that Hemingway's attempt was futile, but that it seems it is impossible to prepare soldiers fully for war, particularly since the technology for war continues to change.

The novels, posters, and other materials discussed here reveal how literature both participates in and resists the larger cultural machine. But it is usually the case that the resistance comes *after* the experience of the war, and so the resistance becomes resentment and is too late actually to stop the war. Instead, the literature of resentment in the 1920s and 1930s— often known as modernism—is backward looking and often nostalgic for the moment when change *could* have happened. This is not to say that modernism has not offered us a new sense of understanding the world and new forms through which we may perceive the world, but we must understand the underlying premise on which this new literature is based: Modernist writers' insistence on change is a reaction to the same system that defined men's and women's pre-war roles and that produced a deep resentment by men against women and a sense of confusion in women about their place in the ideological system.

Literature around the time of World War I has been particularly problematic for critics to categorize, as male writers are often classified as "modernists" and female writers as "realists" or "sentimentalists." More recently, critics such as Suzanne Clark and Michael North, among others, have proposed that male writers defined their work as modernist specifically in opposition to what women writers were doing. North, for example, points out that despite the critical attacks on Willa Cather's *One of Ours,* "few of Cather's contemporary critics have noticed how closely [*One of Ours*] resembles other works published in the same year" (1999, 179). He also suggests that critics rejected the novel because Cather portrayed "a redistribution of human qualities in which even a battlefield might witness behavior that is conventionally feminine" (192), and he concludes that her work showed too closely that what male authors were doing was not rejecting femininity but rather trying to find a way for art and the aesthetic to become masculine. By studying the broad range of literature published in 1922, North reveals conflicts and tensions that male critics have sought to hide, perhaps even from themselves.

Despite resentment or misunderstanding of the opposite gender, women's and men's literature can be remarkably in tune in terms of both content and method, and comprehension of one category of literature, particularly one that seems to be gendered, can lead to greater opportunities of understanding another, especially its "opposite." Rereading texts that seem easily classified has proved invaluable; a close reading of "domestic" and "sentimental" novels shows such texts to have a bearing on "war" novels, and reading domestic ritual within war novels demonstrates these works' engagement with the construct of the home. In both cases, the domestic (in the case of war literature) or political (in the case of domestic literature) details are not incidental, not subplots or minor threads, but rather crucial structures in the works as a whole. This is not to suggest that Boyd's *Through the Wheat* is not a war novel; rather, it is a war novel *because* it talks about battle and *because* it portrays domestic rituals that have been changed by the war, and those alterations themselves show the impersonality and dehumanizing aspect of technological war. Similarly, this rereading does not imply that Glasgow's *Sheltered Life* is not a domestic novel. Instead, the domesticity portrayed in that novel simultaneously creates an ideological framework through which characters understand the war and undermines the foundations of that framework. An inclusive rather than an either/or approach to understanding literature offers tools for scholars of both domestic literature and war literature to broaden their repertoire of ideas about each category and the overlapping nature of both.

Furthermore, a close look at these categories suggests that the process of categorization is, not surprisingly, highly political. A war novel is defined as such because it is about men in battle, learning to navigate changes in their personal worlds that the war reveals. A domestic novel is about women at home, negotiating their society and its demands, often when extreme social change is in process. The primary distinctions, then, are who the novel is about (men or women), what social and political changes they face, and what internal shifts in gender expectations they experience. The structures of these kinds of novels resemble each other closely, and the war novel and the domestic novel often employ similar literary techniques. Thus categorization is highly subjective and reflects what we choose to see and value. By examining our criteria for categorization, we can broaden what we choose to see and subsequently what we choose to value.

This approach can also enliven our understanding of literature in general. Too often, men and women writers are pitted against each other, whether by their own desire, by that of their critics, or by historical cultural viewpoints, but such a sense of combativeness can limit our reading and understanding. A recent issue of *American Literary Studies* centered on the idea of "No More Separate Spheres." Essays there interrogate the long-held notion that nineteenth-century men and women lived in completely different worlds and question whether such an approach is a valuable critical method. This idea of separate spheres bears a closer look, not only about nineteenth-century writing but also about men's and women's writing in general. Although male and female authors both approach topics from different perspectives and use different languages to do so, it is important to recognize that men and women live in the same world, and it is the conjunction and juxtaposition of their experiences that make up that world. This is not to say that men and women arrive at the same conclusions, but literary critics must be prepared to recognize multiple versions of events, sort through those versions, and acknowledge that some questions cannot be answered simply.

Of course, this study has focused only on World War I, a war in which gender roles were still perceived as relatively distinct and rigid. Even though some women went to the front, for the most part men did the fighting. The United States is presently in a different situation, with women participating at the battle front more actively than ever before. The effect of their military work on literature may be profound, as women soldiers tell their tales, which will inevitably include incidents of domestic ritual and attitudes toward the home. Another development will be accounts by male soldiers whose comrades include female soldiers, thus potentially affecting the simple equation of women with home. The shape these narratives will take is yet to be determined, but the constructions of battle front and home front will remain prominent. They may come to take less oppositional stances toward one another, but since war literature to date almost consistently reflects a disenchantment with the ideology established by the home front to accommodate war, it is likely that it will continue to do so. What will happen when women come to resent notions of patriotism and loyalty established and represented, at least ideologically, by other women? Or, with the increasing number of men assuming the primary (and sometimes sole) domestic role, ideas about home may be forced to shift away from an alignment with gender. Such changes and resulting new conflicts may provide a great opportunity for revision of the constructs of both home and war as well as of gender itself and for a new literature that relates them.

Notes

Note to Preface

1. Naturalism too seemed to eclipse the domestic novel. In *"Just a Housewife"* (1987), Glenna Matthews suggests that the domestic novel was dead by the 1860s, replaced by antidomestic works such as Stephen Crane's *Maggie: A Girl of the Streets* (106).

Note to Introduction

1. I am painfully aware that I have included no writers of color in this study. Certainly African Americans wrote about World War I, but the selected writers were more influential in mainstream ideology.

Notes to Chapter 1

1. See David Kennedy, *Over Here: The First World War and American Society* (1980), on the way American mobilization for the war revealed the complex dynamic between business and government.
2. The British justified their blockade of Germany on the grounds that German food controls made civilians as much a part of Germany's battle plan as the soldiers. According to Cooperman, Sir Edward Grey argued that "the German civilian population had accommodated itself to this program and therefore could be regarded as a 'belligerent population' which . . . could be 'starved into submission.' Women and children, in other words, who persisted in eating according to government regulation, would henceforth be considered 'combatants differing only in the weapons they carried'" (1967, 15–16).
3. The Vigilantes, formed late in 1916, were a group of hawkish writers that included Edwin Arlington Robinson, Amy Lowell, Vachel Lindsay, Edgar Lee Masters, George Washington Cable, Hamlin Garland, Gertrude Atherton, and many other authors popular at the time. Many of the members split from the group because of its requirements that members produce

propaganda on demand, but quite a few stayed with the organization throughout the war. (See Van Wienan, 66–67.) The Vigilantes' goals, described in
Literary Digest, were "to drive the peace-at-any-price man to cover, to arouse
the youth of the nation to their duties in peace and war, and to carry on a
propaganda that will thrill the country" (1061). As part of his "reconnais-
sance" for Britain's quiet propaganda campaign to bring the United States into
the war on the side of the Allies, Pomeroy Burton referred to the Vigilantes
as "by far the most important distribution agency" of propaganda; the
Vigilantes were also supported financially by the British (Ross 1996, 80).

    4.   The image of Drusilla corresponds to images of women draped in the
American flag on propaganda posters, discussed earlier.

    5.   African Americans were not allowed to volunteer for the military,
although they were drafted at a higher percentage than whites. They also
made up a high proportion of the labor battalions, doing the menial work of
the war. See David Kennedy (1980, 158–63) on the racism of the U.S. military during World War I.

    6.   Although both Romines and Levy devote much space to Cather in
their studies of domestic writing, neither critic makes much mention of *One
of Ours.* Levy skips the novel altogether. Romines points out the problem
Cather had with housekeeping, having seen the struggle of her mother and
other women to set up housekeeping in the newly settled Nebraska (1992).
In Cather's writing, Romines claims, the male perspective is a way to view
housekeeping from the outside, a position of safety, and thus to romanticize
it; Romines points specifically to the housekeeping scenes in *Death Comes for
the Archbishop.* But *One of Ours* is also a novel fascinated by housekeeping and
the problems it presents—particularly when the housekeeper is a man.

    7.   In the United States, David Kennedy shows, instructors in schools and
universities taught that the goal of the war was to keep Germans from
destroying homes and murdering people (1980, 55).

    8.   Edith Cavell was a British nurse shot by German troops.

    9.   Elshtain makes this point in a disparaging way: "Claude goes from
being one sort of wimp, to use modern parlance, to being another. Claude is
a Beautiful Soul" (1987, 217). Simply mocking Claude and Cather limits the
opportunity to see how the ideologies of home, war, and gender depend on
and interact with each other.

Notes to Chapter 2

    1.   Harold Krebs, home from the war, rejects his mother's love in reaction
to the indifference of American society, which has not welcomed him back
or prepared him to readjust to civilian life.

    2.   Of course there was also a strong antiwar movement that played on
ideas of motherhood. Lyricist Alfred Bryan's 1915 song "I Didn't Raise My Boy
to Be a Soldier," for example, is one piece of popular culture that resisted the

demands of patriotic motherhood. The cover to the sheet music, interestingly enough, reduces the adult son to childhood by depicting him sitting on the floor, clinging to his sitting mother, and protected by her fierce embrace. This image, like those of pro-war images, still reinforces the idea of the strong, influential mother.

3.   G. P. Cather, Willa Cather's cousin who died in the war and on whom she based her character Claude Wheeler, sent one of these pamphlets to his mother. It now resides in the Special Collections at the University of Nebraska at Lincoln.

4.   Wharton's body of writing reflects a conflicted attitude toward the mother figure. Benstock shows that Wharton, contrary to popular belief, did express regret at not having children, but she also points out that Wharton made this statement only after her childbearing years were over (1994, 167). In Wharton's early work, mothers are often negative figures, as Wharton's own was, or else they are absent entirely. R. W. B. Lewis (1975) saw Wharton's attitude toward mothers change as Wharton aged; *A Son at the Front*, he claims, is Wharton's first honest attempt at examining relationships between generations. *Summer*, interestingly, was written in 1917, just before *A Son at the Front*; this work shows an absent mother—two, in fact, for Charity Royall's biological mother turns out to be an alcoholic living on the remote Mountain, and her foster mother dies before the novel starts. When she becomes pregnant, Charity searches for her biological mother and finds her dead, leaving Charity to negotiate for herself what she wants motherhood to mean. She is forced to compromise herself in a marriage to her guardian, yet Wharton ends the novel before facing the question of how Charity mothers her child. *The Mother's Recompense* (1925) attempts to describe absent mothering from the mother's point of view. *A Son at the Front* can be seen as a transition between Charity Royall and Kate Clephane.

5.   In *No Gifts from Chance* Benstock recounts two tales of Wharton's paternity. The first, that she was the daughter of her brothers' tutor, Wharton possibly learned from her brother between 1918 and 1922 (1994, 375). The other story, that she was the daughter of the Scottish baron Henry Peter Brougham, Benstock believes Wharton never heard (9).

Notes to Chapter 3

1.   In his autobiographical *A Moveable Feast*, however, Hemingway disparages Crane: "Tolstoi made the writing of Stephen Crane on the Civil War seem like the brilliant imagining of a sick boy who had never seen war but had only read the battles and chronicles and seen the Brady photographs that I had read and seen at my grandparents' house" (1964, 133).

2.   Leed shows that this kind of ritual bombardment was common and reflected an understanding between the two sides: "The standardized hostility and aggressive hatred that was supposed to define the soldierly character

could not be upheld in a situation in which defensive war had become a way of life. . . . It was common courtesy not to interrupt an enemy's mealtimes with indiscriminate sniping" (1979, 108).

3.   The soldiers' swimming in the Marne, where one of the bloodiest battles of the war had taken place, is reminiscent of Claude Wheeler's bathing in the shell hole. Both are images of soldiers' attempts to clean themselves in tainted water—indications of domesticity turned against them.

4.   When Dos Passos was in Europe, his family and friends sent him articles and essays from the United States, so he knew of the nature of the propaganda campaign there (Ludington 1998, 151).

5.   In his biography of Dos Passos, Townsend Ludington writes that Dos Passos was fascinated by the French ritualization of eating; the scene described here came from a meal Dos Passos actually witnessed (1998, 137).

6.   See Lisa Nanney, *John Dos Passos*, on the impact of industrialization on American daily life (1998, 128–29) and Dos Passos's response. Nanney argues that the text of *Three Soldiers* itself becomes a machine (130). Frederick Hoffman and Jeffrey Walsh also offer discussions of war as machine in *Three Soldiers*.

Notes to Chapter 4

1.   Thomas Strychacz suggests that Tiny may be pregnant because of "her misapprehension of 'Tochter' (daughter) for 'Doctor' and the many references in the story to 'carrying'" (1989, 85n.). I would add that the tension between the couple and the husband's simultaneous concern for his wife's health suggest an unplanned pregnancy.

2.   Hemingway's father, Clarence, wrote a medical essay titled "Sudden Death That May Come to a Recently Delivered Mother," which discusses case histories of women who died unexpectedly after giving birth. Hemingway would certainly have been aware of this essay; see Reynolds, "A *Farewell to Arms*: Doctors in the House of Love" (1996), on Hemingway's familiarity with medicine, particularly obstetrics.

Notes to Chapter 5

1.   David Kennedy points out that most U.S. soldiers who wrote about the war did not discuss the kind of disillusionment that the characters of modernist writers such as Hemingway and Dos Passos experience. Instead, Kennedy shows, the diaries and letters of many U.S. soldiers read like travel writing (1980, 205–6) and reflect the propaganda and ideology heard at home (212).

2.   The failure of the war to facilitate social progress affected African Americans as well as women. Blacks, many of whom had chosen to show sup-

port for the United States during the war, were disappointed by the government's refusal to encourage their attempts to gain positions in the workforce; unions refused to admit them, race riots broke out in St. Louis and Chicago, and lynchings increased in the years after the war (Kennedy 1980, 282–83).

3.   Donald M. Kartiganer (1998), for example, explores Faulkner's treatment of war as a modernist "gesture," a behavior loyal to older codes but also self-mocking, in novels such as *Flags in the Dust, Light in August, The Unvanquished, Intruder in the Dust, A Fable,* and *Absalom! Absalom!*

4.   Frederick Hoffman, for example, comments that Faulkner "portrayed her kind (in Cicely Saunders) in a number of poses ludicrous and pathetic" (1955, 107).

5.   See Michael Kreyling's *Eudora Welty's Achievement of Order* (1980), Albert Devlin's "Meeting the World in *Delta Wedding*" (1989), and Suzanne Marrs's "'The Treasure Most Dearly Regarded': Memory and Imagination in *Delta Wedding*" (1993) for discussions of the growth of "The Delta Cousins" into *Delta Wedding.*

6.   Romines, for example, points to places where Welty exposes the complex relations between black and white women as well as the class system that protects young women such as Dabney but not the girl on the way to Memphis (1997, 225, 226). Danielle Fuller explores the complicated problem of women's sexuality in patriarchal, hierarchical Southern society (1994). And Peggy Whitman Prenshaw argues that Welty's fiction "displays a persistent regard for political negotiations but displaces them from political sites to what we might traditionally call the private sphere, private, perhaps, because these sites are so often the domain of women" (1997, 618).

7.   See also Joseph Childers, "Character and Context: The Paradox of the Family Myth in Eudora Welty's *Delta Wedding*" (1987), on how the Fairchild myth binds family members together.

8.   See Carol J. Adams, who discusses the connections between the First World War and vegetarianism in "Feminism, the Great War, and Modern Vegetarianism" (1989).

9.   Welty was well aware of the danger childbirth posed for women. In *One Writer's Beginnings* she describes how her own mother nearly died after the birth of her first child. Welty emphasizes the impact that learning of this event had on her as a child: Her mother had "told me the wrong secret—not how babies could come but how they could die" (1983, 19).

10.   Westling also pairs George, a Dionysian figure, and Ellen, "whose name by coincidence or design recalls Helen, a Minoan tree-goddess closely associated with Dionysos in the Linear B tables from Mycenaean Pylos and also related to Persephone" (1985, 83).

11.   See Childers on the role of Ellen as outsider instilling the Fairchild myth in her children (1987, 245).

12.   In *Sacred Groves and Ravaged Gardens*, Westling calls *Delta Wedding* "a pastoral hymn of fertility" (1985, 65).

13.   David Kennedy describes the AEF's massive anti-VD campaign that

emphasized abstinence with pamphlets explicitly encouraging masturbation over visiting prostitutes (1980, 186–87); getting venereal disease was a punishable offense in the U.S. army. In Dos Passos's *Three Soldiers* Fuselli is demoted for contracting VD. Other literature such as *One Man's Initiation* suggests soldiers knew about and used prophylactics (Dos Passos 1969, 53, 98).

Bibliography

Abel, Elizabeth, Marianne Hirsch, and Elizabeth Langland, eds. *The Voyage In: Fictions of Female Development*. Hanover, N.H.: University Press of New England, 1983.

Adams, Carol J. "Feminism, the Great War, and Modern Vegetarianism." In *Arms and the Woman: War, Gender, and Literary Representation*. Ed. Helen M. Cooper, Adrienne Auslander Munich, and Susan Merrill Squier. Chapel Hill: University of North Carolina Press, 1989. 244–67.

Aichinger, Peter. *The American Soldier in Fiction, 1880–1963: A History of Attitudes toward Warfare and the Military Establishment*. Ames: Iowa State University Press, 1975.

Alcott, Louisa May. *Little Women*. New York: Bantam, 1983.

Ammons, Elizabeth. *Conflicting Stories: American Women Writers at the Turn into the Twentieth Century*. New York: Oxford University Press, 1992.

Arendt, Hannah. *The Human Condition*. Chicago: University of Chicago Press, 1958.

Armstrong, Nancy, and Leonard Tennenhouse, eds. "Introduction: Representing Violence, or 'How the West Was Won.'" *The Violence of Representation: Literature and the History of Violence*. New York: Routledge, 1989. 1–26.

Auerbach, Nina. *Communities of Women: An Idea in Fiction*. Cambridge, Mass.: Harvard University Press, 1978.

"Authors and Artists as 'Vigilantes.'" *Literary Digest* 54 (April 14, 1917): 1061.

Bailey, Temple. *The Tin Soldier*. Philadelphia: Penn, 1918.

Baker, Carlos. *Ernest Hemingway: A Life Story*. New York: Charles Scribner's Sons, 1969.

Banta, Martha. *Imaging American Women: Idea and Ideals in Cultural History*. New York: Columbia University Press, 1987.

Barlowe, Jamie. "Hemingway's Gender Training." In *A Historical Guide to Ernest Hemingway*. Ed. Linda Wagner-Martin. New York: Oxford University Press, 2000. 117–53.

Bauer, Dale M. *Edith Wharton's Brave New Politics*. Madison: University of Wisconsin Press, 1994.

Baym, Nina. "Melodramas of Beset Manhood: How Theories of American Fiction Exclude Women Authors." In *The New Feminist Criticism: Essays on Women, Literature, and Theory*. Ed. Elaine Showalter. New York: Pantheon, 1985. 63–80.

Beauman, Nicola. "'It Is Not the Place of Women to Talk of Mud': Some Responses by British Women Novelists to World War I." In *Women and World War I: The Written Response*. Ed. Dorothy Goldman. New York: St. Martin's, 1993. 128–49.

Benson, Jackson J. "Patterns of Connection and Their Development in Hemingway's *In Our Time*." Reprinted in *Critical Essays on Ernest Hemingway's In Our Time*. Ed. Michael S. Reynolds. Boston: G. K. Hall, 1983. 103–19.

Benstock, Shari. "Introduction." *A Son at the Front*. DeKalb: Northern Illinois University Press, 1995. vii–xvi.

———. *No Gifts from Chance: A Biography of Edith Wharton*. New York: Scribner's, 1994.

Berlant, Lauren. *The Anatomy of National Fantasy: Hawthorne, Utopia, and Everyday Life*. Chicago: University of Chicago Press, 1991.

Bledsoe, Erik. "Margaret Mitchell's Review of Soldiers' Pay." *Mississippi Quarterly* 49, no. 3 (1996): 591–93.

Blotner, Joseph. *Faulkner: A Biography*. New York: Random, 1984.

Boxwell, D. A. "In Formation: Male Homosocial Desire in Willa Cather's *One of Ours*." In *Eroticism and Containment: Notes from the Flood Plain*. Ed. Carol Siegel and Ann Kibbey. New York: New York University Press, 1994. 285–310.

Boyd, Thomas. *Through the Wheat*. New York: Charles Scribner's Sons, 1923.

Bradford, M. E. "Fairchild as Composite Protagonist in *Delta Wedding*." In *Eudora Welty: Critical Essays*. Ed. Peggy Whitman Prenshaw. Jackson: University Press of Mississippi, 1979. 201–7.

Buitenhuis, Peter. *The Great War of Words: British, American, and Canadian Propaganda and Fiction, 1914–1933*. Vancouver: University of British Columbia Press, 1987.

Bunting, Charles T. "'The Interior World': An Interview with Eudora Welty." Reprinted in *Conversations with Eudora Welty*. Ed. Peggy Whitman Prenshaw. Jackson: University Press of Mississippi, 1984. 40–63.

Campbell, Donna M. *Resisting Regionalism: Gender and Naturalism in American Fiction, 1885–1915*. Athens: Ohio University Press, 1997.

Casey, Janet Galligani. *Dos Passos and the Ideology of the Feminine*. New York: Cambridge University Press, 1998.

Cather, Willa. *One of Ours*. New York: Knopf, 1922.

Childers, Joseph W. "Character and Context: The Paradox of the Family Myth in Eudora Welty's *Delta Wedding*." *Essays in Literature* 14, no. 2 (1987): 241–50.

Clark, Michael. *Dos Passos's Early Fiction, 1912–1938*. Selingsgrove, Penn.: Susquehanna University Press, 1987.

Clark, Suzanne. *Sentimental Modernism: Women Writers and the Revolution of the Word*. Bloomington: Indiana University Press, 1991.

Cobley, Evelyn. *Representing War: Form and Ideology in First World War Narratives*. Buffalo: University of Toronto Press, 1993.

Colley, Iain. *Dos Passos and the Fiction of Despair*. London: Macmillan, 1987.

Condé, Mary. "Payments and Face Values: Edith Wharton's *A Son at the Front*." In *Women's Fiction and the Great War*. Ed. Suzanne Raitt and Trudi Tate. Oxford: Clarendon, 1997.

Cooper, Helen M., Adrienne Auslander Munich, and Susan Merrill Squier, eds. *Arms and the Woman: War, Gender, and Literary Representation*. Chapel Hill: University of North Carolina Press, 1989.

Cooperman, Stanley. *World War I and the American Novel*. Baltimore: Johns Hopkins University Press, 1967.

Crane, Stephen. *The Red Badge of Courage*. New York: Modern Library, 1951.

Creel, George. *How We Advertised America: The First Telling of the Amazing Story of the Committee on Public Information That Carried the Gospel of Americanism to Every Corner of the Globe*. New York: Harper & Brothers, 1920.

Devlin, Albert J. "The Making of *Delta Wedding*, or Doing 'Something Diarmuid Thought I Could Do.'" In *Biographies of Books: The Compositional Histories of Notable American Writings*. Ed. James Barbour and Tom Quirk. Columbia: University of Missouri Press, 1996. 226–61.

———— . "Meeting the World in *Delta Wedding*." In *Critical Essays on Eudora Welty*. Ed. Craig Turner and Lee Emling Harding. Boston: Prentice Hall, 1989. 90–109.

Donaldson, Scott, ed. *New Essays on* A Farewell to Arms. New York: Cambridge University Press, 1990.

Donovan, Josephine. *New England Local Color Literature: A Woman's Tradition*. New York: Frederick Ungar, 1983.

Dos Passos, John. *One Man's Initiation: 1917*. Ithaca, N.Y.: Cornell University Press, 1969.

———— . *Three Soldiers*. New York: Penguin, 1997.

DuPlessis, Rachel Blau. *Writing beyond the Ending: Narrative Strategies of Twentieth-Century Women Writers*. Bloomington: Indiana University Press, 1985.

Elshtain, Jean Bethke. *Women and War*. New York: Basic, 1987.

Fahs, Alice. *The Imagined Civil War: Popular Literature of the North and South, 1861–1865*. Chapel Hill: University of North Carolina Press, 2001.

Faulkner, William. "Literature and War." Reprinted in Michael Millgate. "Faulkner on the Literature of the First World War." In *A Faulkner Miscellany*. Ed. James. B. Meriwether. Jackson: University Press of Mississippi, 1974. 99.

———— . *Soldiers' Pay*. New York: Liveright, 1997.

Fedorko, Kathy A. *Gender and the Gothic in the Fiction of Edith Wharton*. Tuscaloosa: University of Alabama Press, 1995.

Ferber, Edna. "The Maternal Feminine." In *One Basket*. Chicago: People's Book Club, 1947. 94–109.

Ferrero, David J. "Nikki Adams and the Limits of Gender Criticism." *The Hemingway Review* 17, no. 2 (1998): 18–30.

Fetterley, Judith. *The Resisting Reader: A Feminist Approach to American Fiction*. Bloomington: Indiana University Press, 1977.

Fetterley, Judith, and Marjorie Pryse. "Introduction." *American Women Regionalists, 1850–1910: A Norton Anthology*. New York: Norton, 1992. xi–xx.

Flora, Joseph. *Hemingway's Nick Adams*. Baton Rouge: Louisiana State University Press, 1982.

Freud, Sigmund. "Civilization and Its Discontents." Trans. James Strachey. *Civilization, Society, and Religion: Group Psychology, Civilization, and Its Discontents, and Other Works*. New York: Penguin, 1985.

———. "Family Romances." *The Sexual Enlightenment of Children*. New York: Macmillan, 1963a. 41–46.

———. "A Special Type of Object Choice Made by Men." *Sexuality and the Psychology of Love*. New York: Macmillan, 1963b. 49–58.

Fryer, Judith. *Felicitous Space: The Imaginative Structures of Edith Wharton and Willa Cather*. Chapel Hill: University of North Carolina Press, 1986.

Fuller, Danielle. "'Making a Scene': Some Thoughts on Female Sexuality and Marriage in Eudora Welty's *Delta Wedding* and *The Optimist's Daughter*." *Mississippi Quarterly* 48 (1994): 291–318.

Fussell, Paul. *The Great War and Modern Memory*. New York: Oxford University Press, 1975.

Gallagher, Jean. *The World Wars through the Female Gaze*. Carbondale: Southern Illinois University Press, 1998.

Gelfant, Blanche H. "'What Was It . . . ?': The Secret of Family Accord in *One of Ours*." In *Willa Cather: Family, Community, and History (The BYU Symposium)*. Ed. John J. Murphy with Linda Hunter Adams and Paul Rawlins. Provo: Brigham Young University Humanities Publications Center, 1988. 85–102.

Gilbert, Sandra, and Susan Gubar. *No Man's Land: The Place of the Woman Writer in the Twentieth Century: Vol. 1: The War of the Words*. New Haven, Conn.: Yale University Press, 1988.

Glasgow, Ellen. *The Builders*. Garden City, N.Y.: Doubleday, Page, 1919.

———. *The Sheltered Life*. Charlottesville: University Press of Virginia, 1966.

Glenn, Sharlee Mullins. "In and Out the Circle: The Individual and the Clan in Eudora Welty's *Delta Wedding*." *Southern Literary Journal* 22, no. 1 (1989): 50–60.

Godbold, E. Stanly. *Ellen Glasgow and the Woman Within*. Baton Rouge: Louisiana State University Press, 1972.

Goldman, Dorothy. "'Eagles of the West'? American Women Writers and World War I." In *Women and World War I: The Written Response*. Ed. Dorothy Goldman. New York: St. Martin's Press, 1993a. 188–208.

———. ed. *Women and World War I: The Written Response*. New York: St. Martin's Press, 1993b.

———. With Jane Gledhill and Judith Hattaway. *Women Writers and the Great War*. New York: Twayne, 1995.

Goodman, Susan. *Ellen Glasgow: A Biography*. Baltimore: Johns Hopkins University Press, 1998.

———. "Memory and Memoria in *The Sheltered Life*." *Mississippi Quarterly* 49 (1995): 241–54.

Harris, Sharon M., ed. *Redefining the Political Novel: American Women Writers, 1797–1901*. Knoxville: University of Tennessee Press, 1995.

Harrison, Elizabeth Jane. *Female Pastoral: Women Writers Re-Visioning the American South*. Knoxville: University of Tennessee Press, 1991.

Hasbany, Richard. "The Shock of Vision: An Imagist Reading of *In Our Time*." In *Ernest Hemingway: Five Decades of Criticism*. Ed. Linda Welshimer Wagner. East Lansing: Michigan State University Press, 1974. 224–40.

Heilbrun, Carolyn G. *Women's Lives: The View from the Threshold*. Toronto: University of Toronto Press, 1999.

Heller, Adele, and Lois Rudnick. *1915, The Cultural Moment*. New Brunswick, N.J.: Rutgers University Press, 1991.

Hemingway, Clarence. "Sudden Death That May Come to a Recently Delivered Mother." Reprinted in *The Hemingway Review* 18 (1999): 43–45.

Hemingway, Ernest. *A Farewell to Arms*. New York: Macmillan, 1957.

———. *In Our Time*. New York: Charles Scribner's Sons, 1958.

———. ed. *Men at War*. New York: Berkley, 1968.

———. *A Moveable Feast*. New York: Charles Scribner's Sons, 1964.

Higonnet, Margaret Randolph, and Patrice L.-R. Higonnet. "The Double Helix." In *Behind the Lines: Gender and the Two World Wars*. Ed. Margaret Randolph Higonnet et al. New Haven, Conn.: Yale University Press, 1987. 31–47.

Higonnet, Margaret Randolph, et al., eds. *Behind the Lines: Gender and the Two World Wars*. New Haven, Conn.: Yale University Press, 1987.

Hoffman, Frederick J. *The Twenties: American Writing in the Postwar Decade*. New York: Viking, 1955.

Holy Bible. RSV. Nashville: Thomas Nelson, 1963.

Howard, June. "What Is Sentimentality?" *American Literary History* 11, no. 1 (1999): 63–81.

Huston, Nancy. "The Matrix of War: Mothers and Heroes." In *The Female Body in Western Culture*. Ed. Susan Rubin Suleiman. Cambridge, Mass.: Harvard University Press, 1986. 119–36.

Jameson, Fredric. *The Political Unconscious: Narrative as a Socially Symbolic Act*. Ithaca, N.Y.: Cornell University Press, 1981.

Kartiganer, Donald M. "'So I, Who Had Never Had a War . . .': William Faulkner, War, and the Modern Imagination." *Modern Fiction Studies* 44, no. 3 (1998): 619–45.

Kelley, Mary. *Private Woman, Public Stage: Literary Domesticity in Nineteenth-Century America*. New York: Oxford University Press, 1984.

Kennedy, David M. *Over Here: The First World War and American Society*. New York: Oxford University Press, 1980.

Kennedy, Kathleen. *Disloyal Mothers and Scurrilous Citizens: Women and Subversion during World War I*. Bloomington: Indiana University Press, 1999.

Kolodny, Annette. "Dancing through the Minefield: Some Observations on the Theory, Practice, and Politics of a Feminist Literary Criticism." In *The New Feminist Criticism: Essays on Women, Literature, and Theory*. Ed. Elaine Showalter. New York: Pantheon, 1985a. 144–67.

———. "A Map for Rereading: Gender and the Interpretation of Literary Texts." In *The New Feminist Criticism: Essays on Women, Literature, and Theory*. Ed. Elaine Showalter. New York: Pantheon, 1985b. 46–62.

Kreyling, Michael. *Eudora Welty's Achievement of Order*. Baton Rouge: Louisiana State University Press, 1980.

Lamb, Robert Paul. "The Love Song of Harold Krebs: Form, Argument, and Meaning in Hemingway's 'Soldier's Home.'" *The Hemingway Review* 14, no. 2 (1995): 18–36.

Leed, Eric J. *No Man's Land: Combat and Identity in World War I*. New York: Cambridge University Press, 1979.

Levy, Helen Fiddyment. *Fiction of the Home Place*. Jackson: University Press of Mississippi, 1992.

Lewis, R. W. B. *Edith Wharton: A Biography*. New York: Harper and Row, 1975.

Ludington, Townsend. "Introduction." *Three Soldiers*. New York: Penguin, 1997. vii–xix.

———. *John Dos Passos: A Twentieth-Century Odyssey*. New York: Carroll and Graf, 1998.

Marcus, Jane. "Corpus/Corps/Corpse: Writing the Body at War." In *Arms and the Woman: War, Gender, and Literary Representation*. Ed. Helen M. Cooper, Adrienne Auslander Munich, and Susan Merrill Squier. Chapel Hill: University of North Carolina Press, 1989. 124–67.

Marrs, Suzanne. "'The Treasure Most Dearly Regarded': Memory and Imagination in *Delta Wedding*." *Southern Literary Journal* 25 (1993): 79–91.

Marvin, Carolyn, and David W. Ingle. *Blood Sacrifice and the Nation: Totem Rituals and the American Flag*. New York: Cambridge University Press, 1999.

Matthews, Glenna. *"Just a Housewife": The Rise and Fall of Domesticity in America*. New York: Oxford University Press, 1987.

Matthews, Pamela R. *Ellen Glasgow and a Woman's Traditions*. Charlottesville: University Press of Virginia, 1994.

Middleton, Jo Ann. *Willa Cather's Modernism: A Study of Style and Technique*. Rutherford, N.J.: Fairleigh Dickinson University Press, 1990.

Millgate, Michael. "Faulkner on the Literature of the First World War." In *A Faulkner Miscellany*. Ed. James. B. Meriwether. Jackson: University Press of Mississippi, 1974. 98–104.

Nanney, Lisa. *John Dos Passos*. New York: Twayne, 1998.

Nettels, Elsa. *Language and Gender in American Fiction: Howells, James, Wharton, and Cather*. Charlottesville: University Press of Virginia, 1997.

North, Michael. *Reading 1922: A Return to the Scene of the Modern*. New York: Oxford University Press, 1999.

O'Brien, Sharon. "Combat Envy and Survivor Guilt: Willa Cather's 'Manly Battle Yarn.'" In *Arms and the Woman: War, Gender, and Literary Representation*. Ed. Helen M. Cooper, Adrienne Auslander Munich, and Susan Merrill Squier. Chapel Hill: University of North Carolina Press, 1989. 184–204.

———. *Willa Cather: The Emerging Voice*. Cambridge, Mass.: Harvard University Press, 1997.

Olin-Ammentorp, Julie. " 'Not Precisely War Stories': Edith Wharton's Short Fiction from the Great War." *Studies in American Fiction* 23, no. 2 (1995): 153–72.

Piehler, Kurt G. "The War Dead and the Gold Star: American Commemoration of the First World War." In *Commemorations: The Politics of National Identity*. Ed. John R. Gillis. Princeton, N.J.: Princeton University Press, 1994. 168–85.

Prenshaw, Peggy Whitman. "The Political Thought of Eudora Welty." *Mississippi Quarterly* 50 (1997): 617–30.

Price, Alan. *The End of the Age of Innocence: Edith Wharton and the First World War*. New York: St. Martin's, 1996.

Raitt, Suzanne, and Trudi Tate, eds. *Women's Fiction and the Great War*. Oxford: Clarendon, 1997.

Ransom, John Crowe. "Delta Fiction." Reprinted in *Critical Essays on Eudora Welty*. Ed. W. Craig Turner and Lee Emling Harding. Boston: Hall, 1989. 71–75.

Raper, Julius Rowan. *From the Sunken Garden: The Fiction of Ellen Glasgow, 1916–1945*. Baton Rouge: Louisiana State University Press, 1980.

Reynolds, Guy. *Willa Cather in Context: Progress, Race, Empire*. New York: St. Martin's, 1996.

Reynolds, Michael. "*A Farewell to Arms*: Doctors in the House of Love." In *The Cambridge Companion to Hemingway*. Ed. Scott Donaldson. Cambridge: Cambridge University Press, 1996. 109–27.

———. *Hemingway's First War: The Making of* A Farewell to Arms. Princeton, N.J.: Princeton University Press, 1976.

Richmond, Grace S. *The Whistling Mother*. New York: Doubleday, Page, 1917.

Romines, Ann. *The Home Plot: Women, Writing, and Domestic Ritual*. Amherst: University of Massachusetts Press, 1992.

———. "Reading the Cakes: *Delta Wedding* and the Texts of Southern Women's Culture." *Mississippi Quarterly* 50 (1997): 601–16.

Rosowski, Susan J. *The Voyage Perilous: Willa Cather's Romanticism*. Lincoln: University of Nebraska Press, 1986.

Ross, Stewart Halsey. *Propaganda for War: How the United States Was Conditioned to Fight the Great War of 1914–1918*. London: McFarland, 1996.

Scarry, Elaine. *The Body in Pain: The Making and Unmaking of the World*. New York: Oxford University Press, 1985.

Scoblionko, Andrew. "Subjectivity and Homelessness in *Soldiers' Pay*." *The Faulkner Journal* 8 (1992): 61–71.

Scott, Joan W. "Rewriting History." In *Behind the Lines: Gender and the Two World Wars*. Ed. Margaret Randolph Higonnet, Jane Jenson, Sonya Michel, and Margaret Weitz. New Haven, Conn.: Yale University Press, 1987. 19–30.

Sensibar, Judith L. "'Behind the Lines' in Edith Wharton's *A Son at the Front*: Re-Writing a Masculinist Tradition." In *Wretched Exotic: Essays on Edith Wharton in Europe*. Ed. Katherine Joslin and Alan Price. New York: Lang, 1993. 241–56.

———. "Edith Wharton as Propagandist and Novelist: Competing Visions of 'The Great War.'" In *A Forward Glance: New Essays on Edith Wharton*. Ed. Clare Colquitt, Susan Goodman, and Candace Waid. Newark: University of Delaware Press, 1999. 149–71.

Skaggs, Merrill Maguire. *After the World Broke in Two: The Later Novels of Willa Cather*. Charlottesville: University Press of Virginia, 1990.

Smith-Rosenberg, Carroll. *Disorderly Conduct: Visions of Gender in Victorian America*. New York: Oxford University Press, 1985.

Spanier, Sandra Whipple. "Hemingway's Unknown Soldier: Catherine Barkley, the Critics, and the Great War." In *New Essays on A Farewell to Arms*. Ed. Scott Donaldson. New York: Cambridge University Press, 1990. 75–108.

Spilka, Mark. *Hemingway's Quarrel with Androgyny*. Lincoln: University of Nebraska Press, 1990.

Stengel, Wayne B. "Strength of the Mothers, Weakness of the Fathers: War, Sport, and Sexual Battle in Hemingway's *In Our Time*." *Publications of the Arkansas Philological Association* 20 (1994): 87–103.

Stoneback, H. R. "'Nothing Was Ever Lost': Another Look at 'That Marge Business.'" In *Hemingway: Up in Michigan Perspectives*. Ed. Frederic J. Svoboda and Joseph J. Waldmeir. East Lansing: Michigan State University Press, 1995. 59–76.

Stout, Janis P. *Willa Cather: The Writer and Her World*. Charlottesville: University Press of Virginia, 2000.

Strychacz, Thomas. "Dramatizations of Manhood in Hemingway's *In Our Time* and *The Sun Also Rises*." *American Literature* 61 (1989): 245–60.

———. "*In Our Time*, Out of Season." In *The Cambridge Companion to Hemingway*. Ed. Scott Donaldson. Cambridge: Cambridge University Press, 1996. 55–86.

Tompkins, Jane. *Sensational Designs: The Cultural Work of American Fiction, 1790–1860*. New York: Oxford University Press, 1985.

Trilling, Diana. "Fiction in Review." Reprinted in *The Critical Response to Eudora Welty's Fiction*. Ed. Laurie Champion. Westport, Conn.: Greenwood, 1994. 103–5.

Tylee, Claire M. *The Great War and Women's Consciousness: Images of Militarism and Womanhood in Women's Writings, 1914–64*. Iowa City: University of Iowa Press, 1990.

Van Wienen, Mark. "Poetics of the Frugal Housewife: A Modernist Narrative of the Great War and America." *American Literary History* 7 (1995): 55–91.

Wagner, Linda W. *Dos Passos: Artist as American*. Austin: University of Texas Press, 1979.

———. *Ellen Glasgow: Beyond Convention*. Austin: University of Texas Press, 1982.

———, ed. *Ernest Hemingway: Six Decades of Criticism*. East Lansing: Michigan State University Press, 1987.

———. "'Proud and Gently and Friendly': Women in Hemingway's Early Fiction." In *Ernest Hemingway: The Papers of a Writer*. Ed. Bernard Oldsey. New York: Garland, 1981. 63–71.

Walsh, Jeffrey. *American War Literature 1914 to Vietnam*. New York: St. Martin's, 1982.

Welter, Barbara. *Dimity Convictions: The American Woman in the Nineteenth Century*. Athens: Ohio University Press, 1976.

Welty, Eudora. *Delta Wedding*. London: Virago, 1982.

———. *One Writer's Beginnings*. Cambridge, Mass.: Warner, 1983.

Westling, Louise. "Food, Landscape and the Feminine in *Delta Wedding*." *Southern Quarterly* 30 (1992): 29–40.

———. *Sacred Groves and Ravaged Gardens: The Fiction of Eudora Welty, Carson McCullers, and Flannery O'Connor*. Athens: University of Georgia Press, 1985.

Wharton, Edith. *A Backward Glance*. New York: Charles Scribner's Sons, 1964.

———. *The Mother's Recompense*. New York: Charles Scribner's Sons, 1986.

———. *A Son at the Front*. New York: Charles Scribner's Sons, 1923.

———. *Summer*. New York: Collier, 1917.

Woodress, James. *Willa Cather: A Literary Life*. Lincoln: University of Nebraska Press, 1987.

Yaeger, Patricia. *Honey-Mad Women: Emancipatory Strategies in Women's Writing*. New York: Columbia University Press, 1988.

Yongue, Patricia Lee. "For Better and for Worse: At Home and at War in *One of Ours*." In *Willa Cather: Family, Community, and History (The BYU Symposium)*. Ed. John J. Murphy with Linda Hunter Adams and Paul Rawlins. Provo: Brigham Young University Humanities Publications Center, 1988. 141–53.

Zeitlin, Michael. "The Passion of Margaret Powers: A Psychoanalytic Reading of *Soldiers' Pay*." *Mississippi Quarterly* 46 (1993): 351–72.

Index

Abel, Elizabeth, xviii
Adams, Carol J., 127n. 8
advertising, 2
African Americans. *See* race and racism
Aichinger, Peter, 8
alcohol, 9, 13, 18, 20, 73, 80, 99, 110
Alcott, Louisa May: *Little Women*, xx, 22
Aldrich, Mildred, xviii
American Literary Studies, 122
American literature, x, xiii, xv–xvi, xviii, xxi–xxii
Ammons, Elizabeth, xi–xii
Anderson, Henry, 17
Andrews, Mary Raymond Shipman, xvi
Armstrong, Nancy, 58–59, 64, 78
artists: in *A Son at the Front*, 44, 46, 48–49, 51–52, 53; women writers as, xi
Army Air Corps, 106
Atherton, Gertrude, 123n. 3
automobiles: and women, xiv, 28, 114

Bailey, Temple, xvi, xviii, xxii, xxvi–xxvii, 11, 17, 30; Derry Drake, 9–15, 30, 33, 41, 117; Jean McKenzie, 9–15, 19, 30, 33, 41, 117; *The Tin Soldier*, xxii, xxvi, 8–17, 20, 21, 27, 29, 31, 33, 36, 37, 107. *See also* family; marriage; pregnancy and childbirth; race

and racism; sentimental novel; war ideology; war propaganda
Banta, Martha, 2
Barlowe, Jamie, 79–80
Baym, Nina, x, xiii, xvi
Beauman, Nicola, xvii, xviii
"Beautiful Soul." *See* Elshtain, Jean Bethke
Belgium, xxiv, 4, 27, 108
Bennett, Anne Virginia, 17
Benson, Jackson J., 81
Benstock, Shari, 43, 44, 49–50, 52, 53, 125n. 5
Berlant, Lauren, xiii
birth control, 127n. 13; in *Delta Wedding*, 114; hints of in *A Farewell to Arms*, 90
Bloom, Harold, x
Boxwell, D. A., 25, 28, 29, 60
Boyd, Thomas, xvii, 80; *Through the Wheat*, xvi–xvii, xxvii, 34, 59, 64–68, 69, 79, 80, 94, 118, 121. *See also* domesticity and domestic ritual; family; fathers; food; Germans; home; masculinity; mothers; violence
Bradford, M. E., 115
Brady, Matthew, 60, 125n. 1
Britain, 2, 3; British women, 11; World War I literature, xvii, xxii, 51. *See also* war propaganda
Brougham, Henry Peter, 125n. 5
Bryce Report, 3
Bryce, Viscount James, 3
Builders, The. See Glasgow, Ellen

Richmond, Grace, 33; *The Whistling Mother*, xxvii, 33–38, 41, 42, 45, 51, 52
Robinson, Edward Arlington, 123n. 3
Robinson, John, 106
Romines, Ann, xii–xiii, xiv–xv, xvii, xviii, xxii–xxiv, 55, 66, 107, 114, 117, 124n. 6, 127n. 6
Roosevelt, Theodore, 31, 34
Rosowski, Susan, 29, 38, 41, 42, 60, 61, 64
Ross, Stewart Halsey, 3–4, 6, 31, 124n. 3
Royal Air Force of Canada, 98
Russell, Diarmuid 106

Scarry, Elaine, 57, 67, 78
Scoblionoko, Andrew, 101
Scott, Joan, 96
Sensibar, Judith, 43, 45, 48, 49, 50–51
sentimental novel, xiv, xvi, xviii, 55, 93, 120, 121; *Tin Soldier* as, 8–9, 11, 16
Sheltered Life, The. See Glasgow, Ellen
Sinclair, May, xvii
Smith-Rosenberg, Carroll, 1
Socialist Party, 7, 22
"Soldier's Home." See Hemingway, Ernest.
soldiers, 55–58; effect of Civil War on, xv, xx, 95, 119; disillusionment of, xv–xvi, xxii, xxiv, xxvi, 55, 94, 95, 119–120; attitude toward home, xxv, 57–58; experience in World War I, xxi–xxii; feminization of, xxv, 56, 58–59, 60, 73–74, 96, 119; in novels, xv; relationship with enemy, 57, 62, 65, 70–71, 73, 125n. 2; veterans,

93–97, 98–100, 116; writing, xvii, xxiii, 58–59, 126n. 1. See also family; mothers; psychological trauma; war propaganda
Soldiers' Pay. See Faulkner, William
Son at the Front, A. See Wharton, Edith
Spanier, Sandra Whipple, 89, 91
Spilka, Mark 79
Squier, Susan Merrill, xxi
Stein, Gertrude, xi, xviii
Stengel, Wayne B., 81, 83
Stoneback, H. R., 82
Stout, Janis, 40–41, 60
Stowe, Harriet Beecher, xi
Strychacz, Thomas, 126n. 1
suffrage movement, xxv–xxvi, 22–23, 32, 33, 96

technology, xv; and home, xiv; and modernism, xiv; in *One of Ours*, 27; and World War I, xv, xxvi, 58–59, 64, 87, 89, 118–19, 120; in *Three Soldiers*, 74, 75. See also automobiles
Tennenhouse, Leonard, 58–59, 64, 78
Three Soldiers. See Dos Passos, John
Through the Wheat. See Boyd, Thomas
Tompkins, Jane, xii, 9
travel writing, xxiii
trench warfare, xxvi, 7, 58–59, 71
Trilling, Diana, 106, 107
Tylee, Claire, xvii

United States Food Administration, 7

Van Wienen, Mark, 7, 124n. 3
veterans. See soldiers; Hemingway, Ernest: "Soldier's Home"

as Hemingway heroes, 82, 91–92; idealization of, 1, 10, 22; in *One Man's Initiation*, 71–72; as representatives of culture, xvi, 4, 8, 22, 42, 78; and sentimentalism, xiv; soldiers' resentment of, xxvi, 78, 79, 119; in *Three Soldiers*, 76; participation in World War I, xvii, xxi, xxvi, 4, 7, 8, 9, 10, 11, 18–19, 119; role in home, 1, 7, 10–11, 17–18, 19, 111; war fought to protect, 4, 10, 11, 27, 30; war widows, 108. *See also* automobiles; Elshtain, Jean Bethke; family; food; modernism; mothers; pregnancy and childbirth; rape; suffrage movement; war ideology; war propaganda

women writers, x–xv, xvi, xvii, xviii, xxiii–xxiv, xxvi, 14; and *bildingsroman*, xviii; writing propaganda for war, 7, 8

women's work, xxii, 1, 7, 10, 13, 15; as ideological equivalent of men's soldiering, xxii, 7, 14, 15, 16, 19, 30, 36; women's duty, 19–20

Woolf, Virginia, xvii

World War I: as destroyer of civilization, 47, 67, 78; effect on language, xvi, 53, 58, 70, 99–100, 101; effect on Oedipal triangle, 34–37; effect on writing, xiv, xv; seduction of, 69; U. S. participation in, xxi, xxiv, 2–3, 5, 20, 21; U. S. understanding of, xxiv, 30, 95. *See also* civilization; domesticity and domestic ritual; family; incest; technology; war propaganda; women

World War II, 106, 120

Yongue, Patricia Lee, 28, 29–30, 61

Young Men's Christian Association (YMCA), 34, 56, 67, 77. *See also* "Mother's Day, 1918"

Zeitlin, Michael, 102, 103